Hope you enjoy
this book.
Helen
x ♡

EMPTINESS

EMPTINESS
The Beauty and Wisdom of Absence

David Arthur Auten

CASCADE *Books* · Eugene, Oregon

EMPTINESS
The Beauty and Wisdom of Absence

Cascade Books
An Imprint of Wipf and Stock Publishers
199 W. 8th Ave., Suite 3
Eugene, OR 97401

www.wipfandstock.com

PAPERBACK ISBN: 978-1-5326-1061-5
HARDCOVER ISBN: 978-1-5326-1063-9
EBOOK ISBN: 978-1-5326-1062-2

Cataloguing-in-Publication data:

Names: Auten, David Arthur.

Title: Emptiness : the beauty and wisdom of absence / David Arthur Auten.

Description: Eugene, OR: Cascade Books, 2017 | Includes bibliographical references.

Identifiers: ISBN 978-1-5326-1061-5 (paperback) | ISBN 978-1-5326-1063-9 (hardcover) | ISBN 978-1-5326-1062-2 (ebook)

Subjects: LCSH: Nothing (Philosophy) | Christianity Philosophy | Religion Philosophy

Classification: BR100 .A99 2017 (paperback) | BR100 (ebook)

Manufactured in the U.S.A.   10/13/17

CONTENTS

PROLOGUE

This is a book about nothing.

I am painfully aware of the implicit contradiction I have had to accept in writing this, and likewise of the contradiction you as the reader must accept here. For a true book about nothing would be comprised of nothing at all. It would be a non-textual text, a text very difficult to get your hands on indeed. The only difference between such a non-textual text, and having written nothing at all, would be the *indication* of such a text, something that I suppose you and I would have to take on faith as existing at all. The emphasis of these introductory words, therefore, must be that this is a book *about* nothing.

To quickly get your bearings as to what a book about "nothing" could possibly entail, recall for a moment the profound historical significance of the number zero. Think of Meister Eckhart's famous theological dictum that God is No-thing. More simply, think of how useful your cup is every time you drink from it precisely because of the *space* inside that allows you to fill it with whatever delicious beverage you choose. When we make healthy food choices these days, we not only look at the substance and ingredients of our products but also at what is absent ("gluten free," "MSG free," etc.). When we have a conversation with someone, the importance of what we discuss is marked as much by what is *not* said as by what *is* said. Indeed, if it were not for the space in between these very words, this paragraph would be nothing more than a jabberwocky, an indecipherable hodgepodge of nonstop letters. *Absence is significant*. Absence is both a bountiful and subtle experience that permeates our lives, deeply, and in ways that are both dark and bright. Over the years in my own life as a teacher, husband, father, and pastor I have often felt the force of absence whenever I have left a church behind, or lost a friend along the way. Such experiences leave a void in us for a time and then some. Yet, I have also felt surprisingly surrounded by the specter of absence in the midst of utterly sublime moments of prayer and meditation, overwhelmed by the presence of God in a way that I've only known in solitude, absent the presence of others and absent the noise and commotion of the world.

In the New Testament we see that emptiness lies at the heart of Jesus—who he is and what he is about. Scripture tells us, "In your relationships with one another, have the same mindset as Christ Jesus: who, being in very nature God, did not consider equality with God something to be used to his own advantage; rather, he made himself *nothing* by taking the very nature of a servant, being made in human likeness."[1]

These verses compose a portion of what scholars believe to be an early Christ-hymn sung by disciples during nascent Christianity. I take this to be an especially significant passage for that reason, for what we sing about so often conveys the deepest sentiments and convictions of the heart. Read now the English Standard Version of the same words as compared to the previous translation from the New International Version: "Have this mind among yourselves, which is yours in Christ Jesus, who, though he was in the form of God, did not count equality with God a thing to be grasped, but *emptied* himself, by taking the form of a servant, being born in the likeness of men."[2]

Jesus "emptied" himself, it says. He made himself "nothing." The Greek word used in the text for the idea of emptiness and nothingness is *kenosis*. To embrace the way of *kenosis*, like Jesus,

1. Phil 2:5–7, italics added.
2. Ibid., italics added.

is to regard nothing as a virtue. This is a foreign notion for too many of us in a society that still very much prides its individuals on making "something" of themselves. To be made nothing, to empty oneself, this is strange wisdom indeed.

A friend suggested to me the other day that "emptiness" doesn't really have any positive associations, at least not in how it immediately strikes us. Ostensibly, it comes across as a downer. That might be true. But even if this is the weighted connotation of the word "emptiness" for too many of us today, it is for precisely this reason that we need to take with the utmost seriousness the biblical challenge to the degradation of the meaning of emptiness which, according to Scripture, is a sublime and central reality for us to know, and practice, according to the model set before us in the Christ, the one who emptied himself (*kenosis*) and in so doing showed us a better way, what early Christians referred to as "the Way." It is a strange yet beautiful Way. This Way is the opposite of being full of your self. It is a Way of embracing the empty, and emptying your self, in order to be full of Another, so that we might be more fully committed to the others who need us in this world.

We might begin to shift the negative paradigm we have in mind for emptiness by remembering this: contemporary science has revealed to us that 99.9% of all matter is, in fact, empty space. All of the things around us that look and feel so solid are, in truth, made up primarily of nothing, as the British physicist Sir Arthur Eddington discovered in the early twentieth century. This fact, taken in tandem with the fact that the vast majority of the universe is composed of space beyond space and yet more space, should arrest our attention. If so much of the universe is so essentially constituted by emptiness, then perhaps there is something deeply significant about absence, despite our first impressions.

Why do we typically ignore space? It's all around us. Just because we can't see the empty doesn't mean there isn't any value to it. Quite the opposite in fact. Two objects cannot occupy the same space at the same time. Without space, there would be no place for you to be. Absence in this way, and others, is quintessential. This book seeks to correct our neglect of absence and even to plumb its wisdom.

I am working from three primary sources here, at times cited explicitly and at other times operative in the text implicitly: the Celtic wisdom of John O'Donohue, the Taoist wisdom of Lao Tzu and Chuang Tzu, and especially the Judeo-Christian wisdom of the Bible. If you are a person of Christian faith reading this and the first two of this trinity of sources causes you to raise an eyebrow, it is good to remember that *God is big*. The inimitable words of Saint Augustine are worth keeping in mind. Augustine taught "that which is called the Christian religion existed among the ancients and never did not exist from the beginning of the human race until Christ came in the flesh."[3] These are important words about where and how God touches our lives coming from arguably the single most influential person ever to shape the Christian faith since the canonization of the Bible. Augustine says in effect, "Open your eyes!" Faith is for seeing, seeing God, in more and more places. God *is* God, after all, uncontainable, uncircumscribable, *big*, and God has never left us alone.[4]

The religious wisdom of both the East and West are united in this conviction about our topic at hand: the mindful individual will contemplate the emptiness of human existence, not as some morbid preoccupation, but as a spiritually edifying discipline.[5] To that end, this is an original text through and through. Yet these meditations for you, my reader, are much less concerned with originality per se and more concerned with weaving together insight, with an eye toward helping us to enjoy and explore emptiness. I am comforted to know that I am not alone in this style of approach. The French essayist Michel de Montaigne in the sixteenth century thought of his own musings less as works of originality and more as a thoughtful composite of insights from great minds, like a bee going to collect pollen from beautiful flowers to make his sweet honey. The scholastics of the medieval period, similarly, such as

3. Augustine, *Of True Religion*, 10.

4. Ps 139; Rom 1:20.

5. Raposa, *Boredom and the Religious Imagination*, 48.

Saint Bonaventure, thought of themselves not as innovators, but as compilers or weavers of approved opinions.[6] Indeed, some of the best thinking in Christian theology has come as a result of pairing Scripture with good conversation partners. Plato for Saint Augustine and Aristotle for Saint Thomas Aquinas come to mind. In a similar fashion, I am bringing together Christian thought with Taoist and Celtic thought to help us probe the surprisingly life-giving realm of the empty.

Please know from the start that this book is not an argument. I am not interested in trying to "prove" to you this or that, which, ultimately, depending on your life experience thus far, you may or may not be so inclined to believe. I have taken good advice to heart from John O'Donohue about what is (and is not) worth writing. Most research tries to establish a convincing conclusion or reach verifications that no one can successfully criticize or undermine. It's all about argument and arguing (something). Many take this path. There is nothing new in it. Better instead is to take a different approach: discover a few key questions in an area of inquiry not many have thought of asking. Then you create something vitally different, intriguing, and life-giving.[7]

Why do we tend to take space for granted? Do we miss something important when we ignore the empty? What is the "substance" of absence? These are my questions.

The following chapters addressing these questions I would suggest are best read as a devotional. Devotions to be sure are a lovely idea in the religious imagination. To be devoted to something is to be in love with something, or someone, and marking out time in our days for devotions ensures that we have space and time for love, loyalty, and passion. This devotional text is romantically designed to spark reflection, and especially to fan into flame the gift that you are. Beyond reflection, these devotions are intended as much for practical use as for thought. I agree with Soren Kierkegaard who once said "the highest and most beautiful things in life are not to be heard about, nor read about, nor seen but, if one

6. Manguel, *Curiosity*, 49–64.

7. O'Donohue, *Anam Cara*, 145–46.

will, are to be lived."[8] Though you can read this devotional straight through without stopping, I recommend reading no more than a meditation a day. Take time to stop, allowing space between each reading. The space is important. And, where possible, experiment with application. *Enjoy* experimenting. You will reap much more from it if you do, and that is very much my hope for you.

I also highly recommend reading these meditations, if at all possible, in the morning. Morning is a glorious time of pain and potential as we traverse the threshold of sleep, struggling to come out of the unconscious and into the conscious realm of light and life where great things can happen in us and through us in the day ahead if we first take the time to center ourselves in what matters most. The orientation of your heart at the day's break is key to living a life of hope, faith, and love that transfigures our lives as much as the lives of those around us. So, enjoy a few moments of reflection and meditation, allowing these meditations to guide you, early, alone, *absent* of others and noise, in what Jesus called the secret place of the Most High.[9] This was his practice, and hey, if it was good enough for Jesus, there's probably something really good in it for us.[10]

---

8. Kierkegaard, *Either/Or*, 89.

9. Matt 6:5–6; cf. Ps 91:1.

10. Mark 1:35; Luke 5:16.

WHY I BURNED MY BOOKS

When we hear the word holocaust we default to thinking about the atrocities of what the Nazis did to the Jews during World War II. But the term has a more ancient meaning that transcends only that association. Holocaust originally was a sacrificial act and term used by the people of Israel during what Christians call the Old Testament period. It referred to the complete eradication of something by fire, as in animal sacrifices performed as part of the Old Testament covenant between Yahweh (God) and the people of God. It was an offering, a way of transforming something into smoke and mist, towards a nothingness, erasing that thing from its current form of presence here on earth that it might be graciously given back to the One from whom all things come. Indeed, true generosity is often motivated by just such an awareness, namely, that there is no thing that is a "thing" which has not in some way, shape, or form been given to us by something or Someone other than us. All we have, all that *is*, is given. There is a "givenness" to life. Everything is grace. To recognize this, and to remember this (the remembering is key), leads us to a place of living more generously. Sacrificial acts among the ancient Israelites were one way of expressing gratitude and generosity.

When I entered into my fifth year of ministry with the First Congregational Church of Ramona, California where I serve as pastor and teacher, I felt what I can only describe as a strange sacrificial emptying, a shift, happening within. FCC is a remarkable Christian community filled with many gracious people. Going against the grain of the mega-church movement, this congregation prides itself on intimacy, smallness, and connections. You can actually be greeted by name on a Sunday. Imagine that. But FCC is also a community that goes against the grain of the denomination of which it is a part, the United Church of Christ. While the vast majority of UCC churches are hemorrhaging members like there's no tomorrow—and indeed there may not be a tomorrow for many churches that refuse to creatively adapt to the massive cultural shift taking place globally, affecting everything from the ways we relate to other people to the ways people typically regard organized religion with disenchantment—still, despite this, the First Congregational Church here in southern California has been experiencing a steady swelling in membership, attendance, giving, and most importantly, spiritual vitality, something notoriously difficult to measure yet which can be glimpsed quite plainly through the narratives the people naturally find themselves sharing about their experiences of beauty, forgiveness, encouragement, and transformation here at FCC. We are the largest United Church of Christ congregation in the southern association with a heart for missions and a passion for living a life of love.[1]

Yet, notwithstanding all of the good things happening in the life of our humble, traditional congregation—or perhaps because of it—I felt a different kind of *happening* within myself. Instead of the gradual swell the church was experiencing, I sensed a gradual ebbing happening within. It is ironic that when things are difficult in congregational life pastors often find themselves preoccupied by board meetings, heated discussions, working with manipulative personalities, and the like, but when there is a state of shalom and vitality characterizing congregational life such an absence of

1. Eph 5:2.

conflict and challenge can actually usher in a more direct confrontation, not with others, but with one's self.

The inner ebb felt strange and hard to articulate, yet something I came to see had been brewing inside me for some time. Like the beautiful but tumultuous ocean waves I see before me as I write these words while seated on a craggy ledge overlooking the sea in San Diego, so, too, the oceanscape of my inner life had been moving toward a place even beyond ebb and flow and more radically toward a place of absence. For years now I had felt what I would call God's Holy Spirit gently pulling me more and more toward being. Nothing more and nothing less than just that: being. Indeed, learning to *be* with God—to feel the Holy Wind refreshing, moving, and guiding us—is part and parcel of what it means to be on the spiritual journey. The spiritual life is not in the first instance about organized religion, memorizing Bible verses, or knowing more about doctrine or theology or church history than the next guy or gal. It is and always has been in the first instance about *being*—being in, and with, the living God. If we cannot come to *be* more fully at home in ourselves, which is simultaneously coming to be more fully at home in God, then we have done absolutely nothing spiritually except engage in the façade of an external adventure, all the while entirely missing the point of the One who is closer to us than the very air we breathe.

Being, as such, is a thoroughly counter-cultural idea and practice in a world filled with busyness, constant emails, text messages, tweets, notifications, and the seemingly endless proliferation of technology that pretends to make life simpler yet which too often seems to accomplish the very opposite. Some well-intentioned Christians I know and love dearly have too often slipped into the trap of the external, of doing this and doing that, this and there and everywhere, a nonstop whirlwind of activity. Of course faith without the external of our good works is a meaningless faith, as James put it so famously.[2] Yet we have lost something vital as human beings without space for being if we only fill the space in our days with doing.

2. Jas 2:14–17.

The value and virtue of being is something you have to discover for yourself. Reading words *about* it simply won't cut it. There are some spiritual exercises, however, that help.

We might try, for example, approaching ourselves in prayer as strangers to our own being. Maybe we *are* strangers to our own being. Most of us have difficulty awakening to our inner world, especially when our lives have become monotonous. We find it hard to discover something new, interesting, and adventurous if we have become numb to ourselves. Deciding to approach yourself as a complete stranger therefore can be liberating.[3] This is a type of meditation, a first step in awakening once again to your inner life by considering yourself a stranger to your own deepest depths. John O'Donohue suggests that such "meditation helps to break the numbing stranglehold of complacency and familiarity. Gradually, you begin to sense the mystery and magic of yourself. You realize that you are not the helpless owner of a deadened life but rather a temporary guest gifted with blessings and possibilities you could neither invent nor earn."[4]

Being with your own being is important because one of the greatest wellsprings of strength for living is within.[5] When we are estranged from our own being, numbed by familiarity and flooded by a deluge of doing, our inner lives become impoverished. We need to be reacquainted with being, the wellspring of who we are, if we are to live courageously. Strength and courage for living life beyond just going through the motions of our daily routines will well up from within us with passionate ferocity guiding us to see and approach life with wild love and daring creativity the more we learn truly to be.

This is why I burned my books. I recently set fire to the vast majority of my theological library—a kind of holocaust—not as an act of violence, but because I realized a new season was dawning in my life, a season of greater being. To enter into that new season meant letting go of some significant things from the current

3. O'Donohue, *Anam Cara*, 92.

4. Ibid., 92.

5. Luke 17:21; 1 Cor 3:16; 1 John 2:27.

season of my life that had been good for a time, but now needed to fade and fall away. This was the "shift" I had been sensing within. But it was by reacquainting myself, with myself, as a stranger to my own being, which finally allowed this to happen.

After six long years of training in theological rigor through undergraduate and graduate school, and already after more than a decade of devotion to continued study and service within the church, I appreciate all that I've learned through books. But books can only take you so far. And if I am to be honest here (which hopefully I am) after you have finished reading *this* book I recommend that you burn it, in love, or at the very least pass it along to another and rid yourself of it. What you are really craving, what your heart truly longs for, the deepest desires etched into the fabric of your being, cannot be found in a book, not in this book or any other book—*not even the Bible*. Don't freak out that I just said that. I love the Bible. Its wisdom is unparalleled. But even the Bible, with all of its truth and wisdom, is nothing more than words on a page if ultimately it does not move us to connect personally and intimately with the One of whom it speaks so passionately. It is strange that we miss this point so often in reading the Bible, how page after page the Bible points *away* from itself, to the One who is the ground of our being.

I continue to read the Bible regularly, and other books, too, though much more selectively and slowly now in this new season of my life. I will continue to appreciate all that I have gained through the written words of others. But, to switch metaphors, as I am given now to new birth, again,[6] one that I am still feeling out in its entirety and mystery, I know that I've been called to empty myself, of so much past learning, and to engage on a new path of unlearning.

I am reminded of Abba Paul, a desert monk whom John Cassian tells us about in *The Institutes*. Paul would weave these

---

6. Confessions of my original "born again" experience, or what I usually prefer to call my "spiritual awakening" because of the loaded negative connotations too often associated with the former designation, are recounted in *Embrace*, 99–108.

beautiful, intricate baskets day after day as he prayed, and sold them to support his reclusive religious lifestyle. I can only imagine all the hours, effort, and attention to detail that went into creating each one. At the year's end, however, Paul would take all the leftover baskets that had accumulated in his cave and he would burn them. It was a holocaust. A devotional. It was an act of loving detachment, a vivid reminder to himself and others that all things fade, and that's okay.

My wife recently completed a large puzzle by the painter of light Thomas Kinkade that she had been working on for several days at our kitchen table. It was an especially challenging puzzle, not only because of the number of pieces involved but especially because of the details in the picture which involved sea and sky and which therefore seemed to blur the pieces into similarity, making it nearly impossible to distinguish one from another. The very moment Erin finally finished the puzzle, she announced it and then said, "Well, let's put it away now." My children were horrified! "What?" they protested in disbelief. "You can't do that. Leave it out for at least a day for us to see, please," they insisted. Erin did.

This humorous event reminded me of a trip a friend and I took to the University of Oregon one summer to witness a group of Buddhist monks making a mandala. A mandala is an ornate design made up of tiny bits of colorful sand that monks work on continuously until it is completed. In the case of this one, the monks spent more than one hundred consecutive hours creating it, taking shifts, and then, the moment it was completed, they brought the exquisite creation down to the nearby river and swept it all away. It was not a hateful or dismissive act. Rather, it served as a vivid reminder of the transience of life, and that a thing isn't beautiful because it lasts.

After recently completing a retreat in silence and solitude at the Spiritual Ministry Center in San Diego, the first thing I did the following Monday was walk into my office to begin pulling books from my bookshelves. I had clarity about what I needed to do. I tossed the books, with some remorse, one after another, into several large black trash bags. The words of Jesus came drifting to mind during this ritual, "If your eye offends you, pluck it out; if your arm offends you, cut it off."[7] My books didn't quite "offend" me. But their time had come and gone. I had realized I needed to prepare the soil of my soul for a new season. To do that required something that, for me, was *big*. As we're all familiar with, letting go of things in this life—most anything—is terribly difficult. We get attached. We cling. We fiercely hold on to the familiar, even at times to our own detriment, and even death. As I tossed book after book after book into the trash, a couple hundred of them at least, I felt something of the pain that comes with detachment, because it wasn't just books I was discarding. It was also in a way a part of myself. Yet I knew what I had to do. Paul the Apostle would have backed me up. "I consider everything a loss," Paul said, "because of the surpassing worth of knowing Christ Jesus my Lord, for whose sake I have lost all things. I consider them garbage that I may gain Christ."[8]

Did you know that the Bible swears here in this passage? It does. Most popular translations render the word here for "garbage" as just that: "garbage" or "trash." But the actual word (pardon me) is "shit." That's how strongly Paul felt about "everything" he says compared to knowing Christ. Living in Christ, being in Christ, knowing Christ personally, intimately, as *reality* and not just an idea that religious people enjoy talking about from time to time, in Paul's mind, nothing trumps that. Compared to the *being* of Christ, it seemed to Paul that other things just weren't worth comparing, at all. Christ is in an entirely different league. I have to agree with Paul.

So, I threw my books away and in my fireplace at home burned others. It was an emptying. It was an offering. Done in gratitude and out of love. A holocaust of sorts. A claiming *externally* of a shift happening *internally*. Ultimately, it was liberating. It was hard. But it felt right. On my bookshelves now, in place of the many texts once there, I have a small plaque. It says: space is a virtue.

7. Matt 5:29–30.

8. Phil 3:8.

2

SPACE IS A VIRTUE

My wife Erin had just left the house to take our daughter Isabella to the dentist for her annual cleaning. As I was finishing up my work for the day and powering down the computer, I proceeded to walk into my son's bedroom where Joshua was playing happily with his Batman toys on the floor. I wanted to ask him if he'd be interested in going for a hike around the small mountain situated across the street from where we live. He responded enthusiastically and after quickly stuffing a backpack with granola bars, raisins, and a couple bottles of water, off we went.

I live in an area of southern California known as the Valley of the Sun. It's an absolutely breathtaking slice of heaven on earth. God's callings throughout my life have often led me to very unique places, both professionally and personally. Some bright. Some dark. Some joy-filled and some very difficult. But there has always been beauty—something I know I would be impoverished without and that fills me with gratitude. We need beauty and to have eyes for beauty, "we need beauty as deeply as we need love. Beauty is not an extra luxury, an accidental experience that we happen to have if we are lucky. Beauty dwells at the heart of life."[1]

1. O'Donohue, *Divine Beauty*, 60–61.

As Joshua and I walked along holding hands, his little one encompassed in mine, I felt happy to be out in the fresh air after a day spent inside, thankful for the beauty around us and to have this time with my son. Joshua has always been extremely tactile. He loves hugs, kisses, holding hands, wrestling, really anything just to be close. This tenderness of his is complemented by a wildness I have come to admire about him. At times this wildness is expressed in a distaste for following rules and structure, sometimes to the chagrin of me and my wife. Yet Joshua also has another side to his wildness, one that flows from deep within him coloring his perspective on life such that he is often able to see things that others miss by a mile.

As we rounded the corner and began walking up our first incline we decided to play a game. "I'm thinking of something around us that starts with the letter B," I said. "The blue sky?" asked Joshua. "You got it," I said, disappointed and surprised. "That was easy!" Joshua said with as much disdain as he could muster, as if I had just done the dumbest thing ever and now that it was his turn he was going to show me how this game *really* was to be played. "I'm thinking of something . . . around us that starts with the letter C," he said reflectively. "Crab grass? Colored rocks? Calluses on the bottom of our feet?" "No, no, and no," Joshua replied. "Do you give up?" he quickly wanted to know. No, I most certainly did *not* give up. Sure, I had given him the upper hand by picking "blue sky," an act of kindness, I thought, but there was no way I was going to let my seven-year-old outwit me here. I continued to guess for several minutes, straining my eyes all around the path we were traversing, trying to imagine what on earth had caught my son's eyes. Finally, in a moment of despair, I gave up, thinking he surely must have selected something that would not have qualified as legitimate for our game or something that perhaps began with a letter other than C by accident. Joshua revealed his answer with a stoic face, "Cracks." "Cracks?" I asked. "Yeah, look!" he said pointing down to the earth below. Indeed, he was right. There were cracks, small ones and even large ones, all over the place. Joshua had noticed the space, in between the earth, where there was nothing.

"Clever," I said pensively. "Well, I couldn't guess it, so I guess you get to go again." Joshua was very pleased with this. "I'm thinking of something around us that starts with the letter W," he said with an overly large grin. I paused before guessing. "*W? Really?*" I thought to myself. I looked around carefully high and low. There was no water around. The sun was shining down and there were ants crawling along the dirt and there were all sorts of things around us that began with *other* letters but certainly not *W* of all things. After a few weak attempts at a guess, my son graciously decided to offer a clue. I think he felt bad for me because to him the answer was obvious. "Dad! It's all around us! You can't see it, but you can *feel* it," he said. "*Ahhh* . . . but of course, the wind," I replied. And I was right. It was the wind.

Quintessentially this is my son, teaching his old man something new, through the wildly creative eyes of a child, noticing what for me, at first, often is hidden and not obvious in the least, in this case, absence. Cracks—the *space* in between the earth. Wind—the *invisible* force of the air, essential to life as we know it, surrounding us, suffusing us, yet another form of absence in its spaciousness that cannot be grasped.

I don't think it's accidental that the eyes of a child noticed these things. There is something special about us as children before we "mature" into adulthood. This is why Jesus said to his disciples, "Truly I tell you, unless you change and become like little children, you will never enter the kingdom of heaven."[2]

Returning to childlikeness is a most fitting analogy in Jesus' mind for the spiritual life, and so too the wind. "The wind blows wherever it pleases," Jesus tells us. "You hear its sound, but you cannot tell where it comes from or where it is going. So it is with everyone born of the Spirit."[3] Jesus says there is a wind-like wildness, an unpredictability, when you're living life in the Spirit. When you are born of the Spirit, and the Spirit, far from being an afterthought, is the essence and heartbeat of your journey, it produces a mysteriousness that, honestly, is hard to articulate and

2. Matt 18:3.

3. John 3:8.

difficult to grasp, like the wind. The spiritual life is a journey where things are more felt and less seen, where something like the wind may be heard yet no one can predict where it is going or where exactly it came from. The spiritual journey is characterized by a kind of secretiveness, where the inaudible and invisible become normal features of both how life is perceived (as my son was so good at doing on our walk) and of how we are perceived by others, namely, as being in some important ways *different*, and seeing life itself differently.

What do we see, as most valuable, upon walking into a room, perhaps our living room at home or our office at work? We might begin rattling off a litany of thing after thing that we see before us. Rarely, however, if ever, do we notice what my son was so in-tuitively inclined to notice on our afternoon walk—the space, the nothingness, the absence, the emptiness. Yet, without the space in the room that makes *for* the room, there would be no room for anything else in the room at all. Absence is so incredibly valuable in this way that it is the precondition for the presence and value of everything else. We can rightly say the most valuable thing in a room is actually a *non*-thing. It is the absence. Space is a virtue.

The ancient meaning of the Hebrew word salvation is, inter-estingly, "spaciousness." *Yesha* from which we get the name *Yeshua* (literally "God saves"), "Joshua" in the Hebrew of the Old Testa-ment, and the name "Jesus" in the Greek of the New Testament, is a derivative of the older word *yasha* meaning "wide open spaces." Salvation, in other words, has everything to do with absence, with space, as much with the "not" as with the presence of things, people, and the hundreds of activities that characterize the frenetic busyness of our days.

Years ago, in the ancient Mediterranean world, if you worked the land you understood all too well how space is a virtue. When it comes to sowing and reaping, space is literally vital. If you sow two seeds too closely next to one another, the plants in their growing will smother each other out. *That which grows needs space.* This is true not only of plants, but of people. We need nurture but also space to grow. Our salvation is directly linked to having enough space in our lives, and learning to value the space—space simply to *be* and not always to *do*. But it seems that we have forgotten how to be. And the idea of absence having any kind of personal significance, let alone salvific significance, has become a foreign notion indeed.

But absence *is* significant because absence is its own kind of presence. When you pull up at an intersection in your car, for example, the absence of a stop sign there is actually also the presence of an indicator: "go." When someone you love dies, and suddenly you experience the absence of that person who's presence was so richly felt for a season in your life, the absence—even though it is a nothingness—is felt, deeply. Absence in this way is not unlike a warm breeze brushing across your face on a summer afternoon, the emptiness of the air, we hear it, though we don't see it or know where it comes from or where it is going. Absence, we might say, has it's own kind of "weight." Absence has it's *own* kind of significance. Absence, in other words, isn't a nothing, not really. Absence is actually a *something*, something that counts, something that matters *even though we can't see it.* The invisibility of absence is reminiscent of God. It reminds me of Jesus' words about the nature of God's kingdom. "My kingdom," said Jesus, "doesn't consist of what you see around you."[4]

In ancient Greece, describing God as invisible was commonplace. We see it all over the place in Hellenistic writings. Given that the gospels, epistles, and various books of the New Testament were written in a thoroughly Greco-Roman milieu it's not surprising that we find this way of talking about God seeping into the Bible itself. Colossians, for example, famously tells us this: "Christ is the visible image of the invisible God."[5]

These words in Colossians are akin to a Buddhist koan ("what is the sound of one hand clapping?"), designed very much to disorient the rational mind in order to open us to something greater beyond what we can merely think. How can something be the *visible* image of something *invisible*? This mystery, rather than trying

4. John 18:36.
5. Col 1:15.

to analytically pick it apart, serves us better if we simply sit with it, meditatively, prayerfully, and so too with the virtue of space. Space is for enjoying. Don't try too hard to put it underneath the mental microscope. Rather, *be* in it. You of course already *are* in it. But to practice really *being* in it is far different. See for yourself.

This can be done by carving out moments in your day for quiet, for just standing, for just sitting. But you can also accomplish this at the kitchen sink or while driving in your car. All that is required is your awareness and intentionality. An old friend, Bill Giles, from a prior congregation I served, once told me how much he *loved* to mow his lawn. This struck me as odd at first. For me mowing the grass was just housework. But not for Bill. Mowing the lawn was the furthest thing from being a chore for him. He told me it was one of the few places he had discovered where he could have space just to be. Even with the noise of the mower. There he could be alone, and recollect his peace of mind, by virtue of the lovely open spaces in his backyard. For him, that space was transformative, even salvific.

Where is your space?

3

IGNORANCE IS BLISS?

In the 1999 cult classic *The Matrix* there is a disturbingly honest scene that takes place about halfway through the film. We've learned at this point in the science fiction drama that the majority of the human race has been enslaved by machines having become self-aware. After many years of war with humanity, energy sources running low, and solar no longer a viable option for power after humans torch the sky, the artificial intelligence, in order to survive, has created an endgame plan: force humanity to passively become givers of their bioelectrical energy, as a power source for the needs of the machines, by creating an illusory world for them called the Matrix. The Matrix is a dream world that *seems* like the real world. The Matrix forces an *experience* on people of the world as it was known at the end of the twentieth century. There are families playing happily at the park and city streets busy with the traffic of life. There are teachers, lawyers, carpenters, doctors, and the like traversing a seemingly rather normal world. People experience in their minds the world as they once knew it with all of its relative joys, thinking they are more or less content, all the while sedated in a lie, their bodies unknowingly plugged into futuristic outlets to feed the machines power for their continued domination of the world. The Matrix is perceived as "normal" life. In truth, it is a fiction and a prison.

There is a human remnant, however, that has never been captured by the machines. This remnant has made it their mission to rescue those still plugged into the duping mechanism of the Matrix. But not everyone can be unplugged so easily. Moving from a comfortable illusion into the hard light of the truth is a shock to the psyche. Like Plato's allegory of the cave, the shock of coming out of the cave, out of the Matrix, is simply too much for some people to bear. Truth hurts. Trading in, say, on the illusory world of being a successful business man making a six-figure salary, driving a shiny Jaguar, for the cold reality of war, living day-to-day in hiding from vicious mechanized terrors, hoping each day won't be your last, that's a hard sell.

A man by the name of Cipher, who has been successfully freed from the Matrix, decides after a while that the truth of reality isn't worth it. After years of fighting he thinks maybe the Matrix isn't that bad. After all, those in the Matrix are generally quite happy, and who doesn't want to be happy? Does happiness trump truth, or vice versa? For Cipher, the possibility of living once again in a less threatening dream world with fewer problems gives rise to the question: why *choose* suffering? Maybe the truth isn't worth it. Maybe truth isn't all it's cracked up to be. Why choose to suffer in the real world against so much evil, and overwhelmingly discouraging odds, when there's an alternative? Perhaps everyone would be better off surrendering to the Matrix.

Cipher schedules a secret meeting in the Matrix with Mr. Smith, one of the agents of the artificial intelligence, in order to make a deal. He will provide the machines with valuable intel against his fellow humans in exchange for reinsertion into the Matrix—as "somebody important" he says—having his memory erased of this horrible thing called the real world. Cipher wants out. Mr. Smith is happy to oblige. After chatting in a restaurant for a bit, Mr. Smith eagerly prods, "So, do we have a deal?" Cipher, slowly savoring each bite of his steak dinner with the enemy casually replies, "You know . . . I know this steak doesn't exist. I know that when I put it in my mouth, the Matrix is telling my brain that it is juicy, and delicious. After nine years, you know what I realize? Ignorance is bliss."

Is it? Many of us seem like we were happier as children when we were ignorant of so much of life. There's no denying that. Childhood is the classic example of blissful ignorance, a time when we are sheltered from so many of the hard realities of the real world. Life *is* hard, terribly hard. You know this as well as anybody, even though you probably have it better in *numerous* ways than so many other people on the planet right now.

Jesus himself plainly acknowledged the hardness of life. Jesus, who described himself as the way, *truth*, and the life, did not promise his disciples that life would be all sunshine and giggles.[1] He promised the truth.[2] He plainly told them that life, true life, meant denying themselves, taking up their crosses, and following him.[3] Those who follow the Christ can expect joy, they can expect freedom, and they can expect real refreshment for their weary souls.[4] Nevertheless, there is no denying that the way of Jesus is also the way of the cross.

Jesus' way of walking in the truth is costly and joyful, liberating and difficult. And on those days when following him is more costly and difficult, we wonder if ignorance might be a more blissful path. We've all had days where we would like to pull the covers up over our heads to hide from the difficulties "out there" as we conveniently close our eyes to return to a dream world where things are a little more comfortable. To ignore that which is challenging in the world, undesirable in your self, and loathsome in others seems at least from one vantage point to be an easier and happier path. But beyond bliss, is there perhaps also something of truth in ignorance? There is. Though not in the escapist way both Cipher and we sometimes imagine.

1. John 14:6.
2. John 8:32.
3. Matt 16:24.
4. John 15:11; Matt 11:28.

A man in the fifteenth century by the name of Nicholas of Cusa addresses this issue head-on in a small but important book called *On Learned Ignorance*. Cusa tells us that he stumbled upon the notion of ignorance being in some ways a blessing, even as something to aim for if we want to live truthfully and fully, as a revelation from God. Lest you think Cusa too much of an oddball for suggesting something so strange, it is worth pointing out that Cusa's notion of what he calls "learned ignorance" (*docta ignorantia*) can also be found prior to him as far back as Saint Augustine in the fourth and fifth centuries.[5]

Cusa begins his *On Learned Ignorance* by observing how some of the greatest wisdom teachers throughout history have openly acknowledged that ignorance, at bottom, is actually one of the truest things humanity can say about anything it claims to know at all.[6] Socrates, for example, says that he really knows nothing, except that he does not know. The wise man Solomon of ancient Israel declares that all things are difficult and cannot be explained in words. The learning of Job through the refining fires of great suffering culminates in the affirmation that wisdom and understanding ultimately lie hidden from the eyes of all the living. The sage Ecclesiastes shares from his experience, "When I determined to load up on wisdom and examine everything taking place on earth, I realized that if you keep your eyes open day and night without even blinking, you'll still never figure out the meaning of what God is doing on this earth. Search as hard as you like, you're not going to make sense of it. No matter how smart you are, you won't get to the bottom of it."[7] Even Aristotle, in his *Metaphysics*, says that with things apparently most evident by nature we encounter the same difficulty as a night owl trying to look at the sun. Cusa concludes, "If all this is true, since the desire in us for knowledge is not in vain, surely then it is our desire to know that we do not know. If we can attain this completely, we will attain learned ignorance. For nothing more perfect comes to a

5. Nicholas of Cusa, "On Learned Ignorance," 304.

6. Ibid., 87–89.

7. Eccl 8:16–17.

person, even the most zealous in learning, than to be found most learned in the ignorance that is uniquely one's own. One will be the more learned, the more one knows that one is ignorant."[8] One may even be happier as well. As Ecclesiastes says, "for in much wisdom is much vexation, and he who increases knowledge increases sorrow."[9] Ignorance, rightly conceived, rightly has its own bliss. This ignorance, Cusa believes, is especially true of knowing God. "The more profoundly learned we are in this ignorance," Cusa says, "the more closely we draw near truth itself."[10] We draw near to the truth of God not nearly as much by learning as we do by unlearning.

Paul said something very similar in his first letter to the Christians in Corinth: "Those who *think* they know something do not yet know as they ought to know."[11] The Taoist Chuang Tzu put it this way: "You are familiar with the wisdom of those who know, but you have not yet learned the wisdom of those who know not."[12] In other words, as much as learning, unlearning has a vital place in our lives.

Whereas Cipher in *The Matrix* feels he has an either/or choice between truth and ignorance, Cusa shows us that the two are in fact intertwined. It's not just that ignorance is bliss but, more importantly, ignorance is truth. Now *that* is something to ponder! Truth is not only data, facts, and propositions about the "real world." Truth is too bright, beautiful, and bountiful to be contained in mere statements. Truth, deeper down, is the smashing of presumed knowledge. Truth has just as much to do and perhaps even *essentially* to do with unlearning. Not acquiring but just the opposite—letting go.

This is not to say that ignorance is always bliss or that ignorance is the only kind of real knowledge. Cipher's escapism in *The Matrix* clearly makes him the villain. There are facts to be known

8. Nicholas of Cusa, *On Learned Ignorance*, 89.

9. Eccl 1:18.

10. Nicholas of Cusa, *On Learned Ignorance*, 91.

11. 1 Cor 8:2, italics added.

12. Merton, *The Way of Chuang Tzu*, 52–53.

and faced in life. There is even joy to be had in understanding. Yet Cusa's unusual observation is a lovely one, too, that draws our attention to the tenuousness of all we think we know.

In speaking about the Tao, the Chinese equivalent of ultimate truth, or God, the sage Lao Tzu writes, "In the pursuit of learning, every day something is added. In the pursuit of Tao, every day something is dropped."[13] Dropping, letting go, unlearning is the path one wants to be on if one truly desires the truth. Sacred ignorance, in the words of Nicholas of Cusa, teaches us that the more perfect path of approaching the One whom our hearts long for and whom we are restless without is through remotion, that is, removing from our minds and from our lives that which is not necessary and that which is not God.[14]

Remotion is a liberating way to approach your self. A wonderfully practical set of questions to ask in the spirit of Cusa would be: what do I need to unlearn? What would I do well to let go? Are there grudges I am holding on to that I should release? Do I continue to covet and collect things I really don't need? What thought patterns are secretly undoing me each day? How much of what I've read and learned has been of benefit, really? The very idea of letting go is a difficult one for us. We cling to the things of this life. Not only that, we buy into so *many* illusions in life, all of which must be undone, to free us from our self-imposed prisons, to take us back to our beginnings in God.[15] Spirituality in this way has as much to do with unlearning as with learning, as much to do with letting go as with embracing. In some ways returning to ignorance can be both blissful and true. What would you do well to forget?

13. Lao Tzu, *The Tao Te Ching of Lao Tzu*, 48.

14. Nicholas of Cusa, *On Learned Ignorance*, 126.

15. Rohr, *Falling Upward*, 99–100.

4

EX NIHILO

The other morning I attended the Men's Prayer Breakfast at our
church and was unexpectedly given the task of leading the
morning devotional and discussion. Apparently that's what happens when you're the pastor showing up unannounced and the
person who was *supposed* to lead the devotional forgets to show
up. One of the guys pulled me aside to ask if I wouldn't mind making something up "out of nothing." I agreed with some hesitation.

Indeed, such moments are sometimes felt quite anxiously.
"Oh my goodness," we might think to ourselves, "I wasn't prepared
for this! This isn't what I was expecting. What on earth am I going
to do?" But I have learned to gradually increase my appreciation
for life's unplanned moments. There are so very many of them after
all. Why not try to befriend them? The vacuous moments of our
lives can have a surprising fecundity to them.

After agreeing to lead the devotional I took a deep breath to
settle myself into the moment. As I sat down after filling my plate
with some home fries, bacon, and eggs, casually sipping on my coffee, I decided to allow my mind to wander. What would be some
good, wholesome food for thought this morning? As my mind
floated, I tried to resist the temptation to immediately grasp for

something familiar, something I had just used in another setting. Though that would have been easy, I wanted to trust that God had something unique to birth in this moment. "God is light," came drifting to mind as I observed the soft radiance gently entering the room through the window next to me. Such a great verse from the New Testament book of First John as few verses in the Bible describe God with such directness and luminous clarity. The full verse reads: "This is the message we have heard from him and declare to you: God is light; in him there is no darkness at all."[1]

Our discussion was quite wonderful. It was filled with questions, some silent reflection, and shared insight as we talked about how we have each seen this Light in our own lives recently—especially in the midst of a world that is too often filled with far too much darkness. In particular, for me, it was interesting to see how the conversation a few times tended to gravitate towards the dark *rather* than the light, even though we had explicitly stated that we were going to be talking about the latter today and not the former. Darkness is like that though: it has its own kind of gravitas, a gravity that pulls us both in terms of what our minds too often dwell on and in terms of what catches our attention on the news and in the world. Yet this is precisely why being intentional about reflecting and reflecting on the light that *is* God is so wildly important. We need to be people who place the emphasis on the good and on the God we see in the big and small happenings of our lives, lighting up our shadowed circumstances from the inside out.[2] It never ceases to amaze me how despite the fact that Jesus very clearly proclaimed *good news*, what the New Testament word "gospel" literally means, too many of Jesus' followers today seem to be habitually critical, judgmental, or just plain negative, a tragic irony that Christians must be careful to guard themselves against as gospel people.

I was delighted to see how blessed our conversation was with so many people who were happy to share and sink their teeth into not only a scrumptious breakfast but likewise the nourishment of

1. 1 John 1:5.
2. Phil 4:8.

God's Word. God provided for us this morning. And this enjoyable "something" came to us as an unexpected gift, out of what at first appeared to be a dilemma, an absence, a "nothing."

The Bible reminds us that God tends to work in just this way. In the first book of the Bible, in the very first verse of the first chapter, something happens at the dawn of creation that many of us miss but which we do well to notice. "In the beginning God created the heavens and the earth," it says.[3]

Notice, first, just before the famous words "In the beginning" there is space. There is a space before the first letter "I" in the word "In" and there is likewise space there on the page to allow that first letter to be written at all. Indeed, were it not for this space on the parchment or paper or digital format we have before our eyes there would be no possibility of writing about, acknowledging, or having a "beginning." A beginning, which is a something, requires space to inscribe that into, a nothing, whether in textual form, or even personally when we are trying to begin something new in our lives. Space is required. Two objects cannot occupy the same space at the same time. If we want to introduce something novel into our lives without risking burnout or overdoing, first what we need to do is to erase something, to create space. Space is gracious. *Nothing* allows for *something*. This in part is the logic behind the classical theological doctrine *ex nihilo*, a Latin phrase meaning "out of nothing," the belief that God created the world out of nothing. Some Christian thinkers like Augustine and John Calvin have read the first verse of Genesis in just this way. God created everything that now is out of nothing that once was. Nothing is the original state of everything, or, as the Tao Te Ching puts it, everything comes from being, but being comes from emptiness.[4]

Simply put, making something out of nothing is what God does. As creatures made in the image of this God we are able to do the same. Rather than fearing the empty, vacuous, unplanned moments that "pop" into our lives, a better response, and one that resonates with something etched deeply within us, is to welcome

3. Gen 1:1.

4. Lao Tzu, *The Tao Te Ching of Lao Tzu*, 40.

the space, and to see what good things might come forth from that space.

Notice in Genesis, secondly, that even if we reject this way of reading the first verse through the lens of the classical doctrine of *ex nihilo* in favor of a more strictly literal interpretation of the text in context with the other following verses—which some prefer— we still see the virtue of nothing there in the text, albeit slightly differently. The second verse in Genesis reads: "Now the earth was formless and empty, darkness was over the surface of the deep, and the Spirit of God was hovering over the waters."[5] In the beginning, prior to there being earth, vegetation, animals, sky, or anything of the like,[6] this early creation nothingness actually has a kind of "substance" to it, or so the narrative can be read. The text says there is a "formless, emptiness" in the beginning in which there exists darkness and water. How very interesting. Water and darkness are, somehow, already there in the beginning as God creates. *Darkness . . . water . . .* just like in a mother's womb.

It seems beyond coincidental that these two *particular* elements are highlighted in the creative moment of the cosmos. Perhaps the Word of God is trying to teach us something here. Life is pregnant with possibility. Creation is continually ready to birth divine things. As a part of creation, we can play a role in that. Especially as we learn to honor the void. We do well to make room: for spontaneity, novelty, creativity, messiness, the unexpected, indeed, for life. Even when we don't make room for such creative moments *ex nihilo* life has a way of hurling us into the void anyway.

In January of 1975, in Germany, a teenage girl had somehow managed through great effort to arrange for the Cologne Opera House to host for one evening the American musician Keith Jarrett. The evening of jazz, played on the piano by Jarrett, would be heard by more than one thousand people soon to fill the auditorium. Jarrett showed up at the Cologne a few hours early to prepare for what promised to be a spectacular night. But there was a problem. As he sat down at the bench in front of the piano to test a few

5. Gen 1:2.
6. Gen 1:3–31.

notes, he immediately noticed there was something wrong with the piano. He walked around the piano, played a few more notes, and then shuffled over to his producer in the corner to whisper something. The producer told the teenage girl who had worked so hard to arrange the event that, unfortunately, unless they got a new piano, Jarrett was not going to be able to play.

There had been a mix-up at the opera house. Instead of acquiring the piano that Jarrett needed to play, they had accidentally gotten one that had this high, tinny sound. The white notes were out of tune. The black notes were sticking. The pedals were not working properly and the piano itself was not big enough to produce the level of sound required for such a large environment.

Jarrett walked outside to his car. With only hours before the concert was to begin, the teenage girl and those assisting her were freaking out. This was totally unexpected. No one saw it coming and they didn't know what to do about it. Tuning the piano they currently had might have been a quick fix but it was beyond such simple repairs. Acquiring a brand new piano just wasn't going to happen. In a rush of despair, the girl ran outside to Jarrett's car, standing in the pouring rain, pleading with him to *please play anyway*.

To her surprise, though Jarrett was highly reticent at first, he looked over the sopping wet girl and took pity on her saying, "Never forget this. Only for you."

A few hours later Jarrett walked onto the stage, sat down at the unplayable piano, and began to play. Within moments it was clear to everyone that something magical was happening. He was avoiding certain keys, and sticking to other ones, which produced a soothing, serene quality to the melody. And because the piano was so quiet due to its smaller size, he was forced to set up these hard, repetitive riffs to create bass as well. He would even stand up to pound down forcefully on the keys in order to evoke the sound he was looking for. It was an eccentric performance.

The audience loved it, and people since that time continue to love it. The recording that night of Keith Jarrett's performance at the Cologne is the best-selling piano album in history. Jarrett, though at first hesitant, chose to embrace this messy, unexpected opportunity and to make something out of nothing.

5

FAITH AS ABSENCE

Faith is such a rich, beautiful way to live life. Faith opens us to the brilliance of seeing life's abundant color, rather than leaving us to live in the bland mediocrity of a black and white existence. Faith opens us to the possibility of real joy in each new day—joy unexpected, unjustified, small and humble yet potent in the levity it can instantly issue in through a friend's reassuring smile or the nonsensical rhythm of a child singing first thing in the morning. Faith *opens* us. It opens us to a better way of being.

What is faith? In biblical perspective faith is very simply this: "Confidence in what we hope for and assurance about what we do not see."[1] Notice, faith is *not* certainty. Faith is "confidence" and "assurance." It is not certitude or proof. For far too long we have had an obsession in our culture with being "certain" of this or that, an obsession that has often tainted too much of the religious life as much as the secular. But for people of faith this is an especially heinous notion to entertain for faith is precisely that—*faith*—which implies doubt. Faith is most certainly (pun intended) *not* certainty but rather that about which we do not have the whole picture. And, heaven forbid, the moment we think we have the whole picture

1. Heb 11:1.

about God is the very moment religion becomes a sham where humility is supplanted by nothing more than hubris. But for some reason people of faith will sometimes feel embarrassed about who they are on just this point, namely, that *belief* is the basis for their way of life, rather than reason first and foremost or some other perceived to be more "solid" foundation.

Yet, one of the truly wonderful realizations that has been increasingly evident within a variety of fields, including mathematics, science, and epistemology (the study of how we know what we know), is that there really is *no such thing* as a sure foundation for *anything* we claim to know as human beings, not at least a "sure foundation" in the sense of something that is *ultimately* proven and *indubitably* certain.

Take mathematics for example. It is generally assumed that math is one of the surest forms of knowing we have. Of course 2 + 2 = 4, we might say to ourselves. How could there be anything less than absolute certainty in that? But such an appearance of certainty in mathematics is in reality nothing more than that—an appearance. The seventeenth-century Irish philosopher George Berkeley was able to "disprove" the certainty of mathematics (to his own satisfaction) using mathematics itself. Take the following mathematical inconsistency for example:

$$12 \times 0 = 0$$

$$13 \times 0 = 0$$

Therefore: $12 \times 0 = 13 \times 0$

Divide both sides by 0

Therefore: $12 = 13$

This inconsistency can only be fixed if you introduce the rule that you can multiply by zero but not divide by it. But such a rule is arbitrary. It doesn't make sense unless you're applying such a rule just to fix such a problem. Mathematics, despite appearances, is not logically certain. Rather, it is a set of rules that makes sense most of the time that helps us to get along and advance in life. But notice, then, how using math is also a tacit act of faith. It, too, is an act of placing *confidence* and *assurance* in something other as much as it is an act of reason. Berkeley was not the only one to notice this. David Hume noticed it in the eighteenth century, and likewise Jacques Derrida in the last century.[2]

But we don't need Berkeley or Hume or Derrida to notice something that children are just as good at revealing. My friend's little four-year-old daughter revealed this to me one evening.

Erin and I had just finished our small group time of worship and studying Scripture together with some friends and were in the kitchen tidying up when this little girl asked her father, "Why?" She wanted to know *why* her father was cleaning up the kitchen with everyone. The question was an innocent one. There was no malicious intent in it, nor was this the philosopher's "why?" It was a child honestly wondering why we had to clear the kitchen table and clean the dishes. Her father tenderly replied, "If we don't clean the plates they'll still be dirty in the morning and we won't be able to use them." But instead of satisfying the little girl's curiosity, she was inspired. "Why?" she asked again. "Well, if we use dirty plates in the morning then we might get sick." His daughter offered up another, "Why?" To the credit of my friend, he decided to play along with his daughter for a solid *four or five minutes* before finally giving up and sending her into the other room to play with her toys. Yet even though the Q and A came to a halt, notice that it did not have to *necessarily*. The questioning could have gone on.

So what? The "so what" is that questioning—the fact that one *can* continually ask "why?"—reveals that the foundations of what we think we know about anything in this life always seem to depend on something else, and *that* on something else, *ad infinitum*. There is no "certainty" as such, and yet this does not seem to bother most of us in the least. We move on with life! But notice—we move on with life less so with certainty and always with a degree of faith, faith that such and such *is* the case while never knowing for sure that it truly is the case—and that's okay.

Faith in this way is ubiquitous—throughout all of our lives. How sublime! How amazing! How refreshing. Faith is the *absence*

2. Strathern, *Derrida*, 28–29.

of certainty and instead *confidence* in what we hope for and *assurance* about what we do not see. Faith frees us *from* an unnecessary preoccupation with certainty—which is unattainable in this life—and *for* simply living life, living life openly with tentative certainties *and* doubt, provisional answers *and* wondrous questions. Living life with faith is therefore something, in truth, that we all already do, whether knowingly or not, intentionally or not. Doing so intentionally, however, is a real gift to us and to others. Faith opens us to the beautifully ambiguous in life, to the sweetness of mystery, and, ultimately, to God.

6

THE ABSENCE OF CONFLICT

Like most people, I hate conflict. Honestly, who really wants to fight? To be sure there are always some who seem to thirst for conflict and any of us can get lost, even addicted, to the drama we sometimes create for ourselves. But what we long for more deeply and more truly is *shalom*. Simply search your own heart to see if this is not the truth you find there, the deeper longing beyond the aggressor within you. Harmony is what we really seek. There's simply no sweeter combination (to paraphrase Mishka) than peace and love. Jesus for a reason said blessed are the peacemakers.[1]

Yet life is filled with no absence of the opposite of our true yearning. Conflict and the potential for conflict seem to be waiting for us around almost every corner. Sometimes we see the adversity coming. At other times we're blindsided. How we *deal* with conflict in life is tremendously important though because it impinges directly on our happiness and well-being, as well as our ability to live faithfully to Jesus' greatest command to love—even when the loving of others is not simple or easy.

I'll never forget the early stages of launching our small group ministry here at the First Congregational Church of Ramona. It

1. Matt 5:9.

30

was a brand new endeavor, so we proceeded with caution and care. FCC had a long-standing tradition of regular spiritual growth opportunities for children and youth by way of weekly Sunday School classes and a youth ministry. Beyond Sunday worship, however, there had been nothing similarly consistent for adult spiritual formation, save for the occasional Bible class here and there that would happen for a brief time and then come to an end. The idea of launching and maintaining a full-fledged adult education ministry where people could join ongoing groups that focused on building relationships, getting deeper into the Word of God, and using their gifts and abilities in missional opportunities to reflect the love of Christ to our community was a much welcomed idea. Well, I should say it was a welcomed idea by *most*. As with any change, no matter how judiciously one proceeds, there is almost always a minority report with at least one or two dissenters to keep us on our toes.

One such dissenter approached me one evening at the church, during our Maundy Thursday rehearsals nonetheless. "Can this perhaps wait?" I asked. "No I don't think so," the man replied with stern eyes. So I invited him into my office, settled into my chair, and listened as he began to vent. It was hard for me to fathom how anyone, especially a fellow follower of Christ committed to the values of community and spiritual growth, could possibly object to gatherings for our members to go deeper into Scripture, service, and Christian friendship. Yet this is exactly what I heard. In fact, this parishioner was so on edge over this new way of doing things in our congregation that ten minutes into our conversation he issued a threat. I was told in no uncertain terms that if I didn't relent on advancing this small group ministry and revert to doing things "the way we've always done them" then his family would have to leave the church and worship elsewhere.

The last thing I wanted was to lose a family over a difference of opinion. I knew we both loved Christ. We simply had different philosophies about how best to advance the message of Christ's love through the church. "How many churches," I thought to myself, "have been split or even seen their demise because of change and debates over the way things have always been done." This was just silly and I wasn't going to have it—losing this lovely family *or* seeing this vital new educational ministry for our church squashed in its infancy. But could I really have my cake and eat it, too?

I am pleased to say that this family has remained at FCC to this very day *and* our small group ministry has been flourishing now for years. I even learned recently that it's one of the most successful ministries of its type in all of Ramona. Interestingly, what helped to pave the way forward, believe it or not, was absence.

Doing nothing was actually the key to moving forward. *Not* engaging. *Not* giving into the threat but also *not* stifling the growth of our small group ministry. Neither. My approach with this disgruntled churchgoer whom I care for very much was simple: yield (as much as I possibly could). Pride may have tried to persuade me to take a different route. He pushed, and I could have pushed back. But there was no place for ego here. Instead, I did my best out of love to accommodate his wishes and his desires for the church, but without trashing an important ministry for adult spiritual formation that our congregation desperately needed and the majority wanted. I explained to him, out of fairness to everyone else, I simply couldn't halt the ministry but that aside from that I was happy to switch gears to do things his way instead—which in this case meant allowing a "class" instead of a "small group" to be taught for a few months. The class siphoned off energy and attention temporarily from our small group ministry, but it was a small and worthwhile sacrifice in order to honor this man as the church transitioned to a more comprehensive way of helping our adults to grow in their faith. Over the next several months, I prayed and trusted that God would lead this family to the right church, whether that was FCC or elsewhere. I also prayed and trusted that God would continue to nurture the seeds of our nascent small group ministry. Other than that I did nothing else at all. I didn't engage in any further debates on the issue. I didn't try to play politics behind the scenes with our Church Council or Board of Christian Education. I did nothing of the sort. And, ultimately, what happened? Nothing happened. The family chose to stay, realizing how much the church means to them, and the number of small groups continued to gradually grow, gaining momentum over the next year. It was a mutually beneficial resolution, achieved by *not* doing.

This is not the solution to every conceivable conflict. Still, when conflict arises in our relationships—congregational, familial, and otherwise—we too often assume that we *must* engage the fight, when in reality sometimes the best approach is to completely *dis*engage, step back, take a breather, gain a clearer perspective on the matter, identify what's really most important, and then, to approach the situation with the right kind of *doing* or *not* doing.

Though this approach to conflict may sound unusual, it is not novel. This is the tried and true method of what are called "soft form" martial arts, such as jujitsu, which I have studied and practiced for more than twenty years now. Jujitsu (literally "the gentle way") is very much about going with the flow of whatever is happening around you. In jujitsu, the throwing techniques and strikes are anything but literally gentle. The art's true gentleness lies in yielding, giving way to your opponent, whenever possible, as much as possible, so as to redirect a punch or transform an attacker's push into your pull.

Too often in conflict when we put our foot down on an issue, dig our heels in, and insist that *our* way is the way it has to be, tempers flair, hearts break, and conflict deepens. Force against force often makes matters worse. Fire to fire only makes the fire bigger. But, when we let go of the ego a bit, and our undue attachment to doing things *my* way, we begin to see a better, gentler way. Lao Tzu put the principle of gentleness this way: "Men are born soft and supple; dead, they are stiff and hard. Plants are born tender and pliant; dead, they are brittle and dry. Thus whoever is stiff and inflexible is a disciple of death. Whoever is soft and yielding is a disciple of life. The hard and stiff will be broken. The soft and supple will prevail."[2] The Bible in its own vernacular says the same: "A gentle answer turns away wrath, but a harsh word stirs it up."[3]

2. Lao Tzu, *Tao Te Ching*, 76.

3. Prov 15:1.

The next time you find yourself dealing with conflict, before you say or do something you might later regret, first, ask yourself if stepping back and disengaging might be an option. Look for openings and opportunities to yield. Look for opportunities to crucify ego and, instead, to love. Jesus said you're blessed when you can show people how to cooperate instead of compete or fight.[4] We are, after all, according to the Bible, ambassadors for Christ, for better or worse.[5] What kind of ambassador do you want to be? In the midst of a dispute what's a better representation of the way of Christ: insisting on my way or the highway, or, looking for opportunities to lovingly accommodate, just as God lovingly accommodated himself for us when God came to us in Christ? Accommodation is the way of God in Christ. Accommodation only sounds "weak" to our ears if we forget that love is the very best way for us to relate to one another—any other—God, friend, neighbor, and even enemy.[6] Yes, life is hard and filled with no absence of conflict for any of us. Yet, if and when one of the parties in a conflict is willing to yield, disengage, to *be* the absence of conflict, we might be surprised at how often our conflicts work more readily towards resolution and reconciliation.

4. Matt 5:9.

5. 2 Cor 5:20.

6. Luke 6:27–36.

7

NEW EYES

My freshman year of high school I began to see that I couldn't see, not very clearly at least for anything that was farther than ten feet away. I realized I needed eyeglasses. For months I resisted telling my parents. I didn't want to look "nerdy." So I struggled. I struggled to see what my teachers were writing on the blackboard in most of my classes, and I struggled with near daily headaches. My lack of vision directly affected my grades and my well-being. But once I finally conceded the truth to my parents, and got my first pair of glasses, beyond having fewer headaches and being able to read the blackboard, I was genuinely and absolutely *amazed* at how utterly vibrant everything looked around me. Had I really been seeing life so blurred for so long? Apparently I had. And I hadn't even known it, or at least been willing to confess it, or do anything about it.

Beyond optometry, seeing, in a new light, is one of the great gifts of religion. The real voyage of discovery in life, to paraphrase Marcel Proust, consists not in seeking new landscapes but in having new eyes.[1] Quintessentially this is what faith is about. Faith is about having new eyes. Jesus understood this all too well. "No one

1. Proust, *In Search of Lost Time, Volume Five,* 343.

can see the kingdom of God unless they are born again,"[2] Jesus taught.

If we put aside any negative connotations we might have acquired from religious fundamentalists about the idea of being "born again" we might be able to hear Jesus' words with open ears and open hearts. We *need* to hear these important words that way because what Jesus teaches us here is tremendous. Vision, seeing, what is truly most important in this life, more so than anything else, God, and the things of the kingdom of God, that kind of vision is categorically contingent upon being reborn. It depends on reorientation. It means entering into a new way of not only *doing* your life but more significantly a new way of *being* in your life. Though we may shy away from the person who gets in our face to ask, "Have you been born again?" many of us would nevertheless do well to ask ourselves, "Has life become so familiar, routine, and even numbing that I am desperately in need of new eyes?"

Life lacks no abundance of beauty for the eyes to behold. To see is such a gift. No one chooses to be blind or wants to be like the blind leading the blind.[3] If we sense our vision is off, like blind Bartimaeus during the time of Jesus, quite naturally we long for healing so that we can see all the things we've been missing.[4] One of the very beautiful things we're often quite blind to and completely miss is the beauty of space.

Artists have learned to see space, and to attend to space, as something that beckons our acknowledgement and maneuvering. You simply cannot create something pleasing to the eye apart from working with and shifting *distance* between objects, clay, paint, and the like. This is referred to as attending to negative space, that is, the space around and between objects in a composition. Rubin's vase is one of the classic examples of such negative space in which the space around the vase forms the silhouettes of two faces. Attending to negative space equally as much as positive space is considered to be a basic but often overlooked quality of good art.

2. John 3:3.
3. Luke 6:39.
4. Mark 10:46–52.

In garden design using negative space is sometimes referred to as *ma* and in Japanese martial arts paying attention to space in the art of war between combatants is called *maai*. Musical artists have learned to have eyes for negative space as well. It's near impossible to compose something alluring to the ear without well-positioned, thought-out space between the notes and lyrics of a song. The pause, the void, matters.

Attending to space in our conversations is likewise absolutely vital. "You wish to see? Listen," advised Saint Bernard.[5] Whenever I work with couples in counseling the number one issue we come around to time and time again is not just communication in general but specifically the need for more and better listening, which is another way of saying we need more receptive space in our conversations. Space to really listen to what another is saying. But space also to allow deeper thoughts to surface in our conversations that cannot and will not surface when we rush another person's end of the conversation, or blur over something important they shared without any time for it to sink in for both the speaker and listener.

Noticing what is absent or what we make absent in our conversations is just as important. I was having lunch with my brother the other day. With me living on the West Coast and him on the East Coast we realized as we sat down for a bite that we hadn't had any face time for two full years. Afterwards, as I reflected on our conversation, I realized that rather unintentionally we hadn't talked about faith. It's not that this necessarily *had* to be a part of our conversation. But it struck me as curious that it hadn't been a part of our conversation, given who I am, but also given the fact that it often had in past years. Several years ago Dan had attended an Easter service with my wife and I where he gave his life to Christ. Yet, like too many well-intentioned churches that offer altar calls at the end of their worship services, there was no follow-up from the church. Dan had been "saved" and apparently was on his own. So I had made a point to follow-up with my brother myself, despite distance, as any good brother should and as non-intrusively as possible, to see if he was reading the Bible and getting plugged into

5. O'Donohue, *Eternal Echoes*, 55.

a good faith community. The fact that this did *not* surface during our lunch conversation actually felt refreshing (perhaps to both of us). I realized how much I trust what God is doing in my brother's life, and I know the feeling is mutual. Surely we will broach the topic again in the future. I want to encourage him and I want him to encourage me. Indeed, done in the right way, sharing our faith is one of the most important conversations we can and ought to be having more regularly with those we love. Still, absence can be refreshing. Presence can be overdone.

Absence in our conversations is telling, even revelatory. We can learn much by seeing what is missing, or ought to be missing, in our conversations with those we care about. We can likewise learn much by taking a fresh look at what is missing, or ought to be missing, on our calendars.

One afternoon as I was setting up the mats in my dojo here in the San Diego Country Estates where I offer self-defense classes to the community, Kaylee, one of my younger students, showed up for class a few minutes early. Kaylee is seven years old and like so many of her peers has a jam-packed schedule even at her young age: school all day followed by (depending on the day of the week) soccer, gymnastics, Awana Club, church commitments, and, last but not least, my jujitsu class every Tuesday and Thursday. Kaylee looked rather exhausted as she walked through the door on this particular afternoon. I asked her how she was doing. Being in a talkative mood she proceeded to inform me of her many commitments on and on for a minute or two. When she finally finished sharing the litany of activities with me I exclaimed with wide eyes, "Wow! Your life almost sounds busier than mine!" "Yeah," she said with a smile and a sigh. "But Fridays I don't have anything," she quickly added. "Fridays are a *very* important day."

Fridays *would* be a very important day—for any of us who find ourselves in similar shoes. Kaylee has good insight. It's an insight not far removed from the Hebrew understanding of *Shabbat*. The Judeo-Christian tradition has long insisted on the importance of regular intervals of rest, even carving out an entire day. Having at least one day a week for doing nothing is crucial. Why? We need balance. Time for rest and reflection in the midst of the rapidity of life's activities is a necessary counterbalance. If life is all *doing* without time for also *being*, regularly, we miss something. We need the regularity and rejuvenation that comes from the absence of doing. The workaholic self in us may protest. But the better angels of our nature know this to be true. The importance of carving out space and time for non-activity in the Hebrew worldview was considered to be more than just a "good idea." The practice was seen as sacred duty—to oneself as much as one that imitates and honors God. How fascinating to see that it is precisely the *absence* of activity that makes the seventh day of creation a literally *blessed* day.[6] According to Genesis, absence is a blessing.

Why is it that we fail so often to see, let alone appreciate, the sanctity of space? No doubt part of the reason is that space and emptiness are so nebulous. They're easy to miss if we're not careful. Absence, emptiness, and space surround us at every turn throughout each and every day and throughout our lives. Yet emptiness embodies a subtlety because of its invisible quality and quantity. Taoist thought for this reason insists that we adjust our gaze, lest we miss the gift of the empty right before us: "We shape clay into a pot, but it is the emptiness inside that holds whatever we want. We hammer wood for a house, but it is the inner space that makes it livable."[7] A bowl is useful because of the space inside it. There is the possibility of planets in the cosmos which can sustain life like our own because of the vacuum of space. Quietly, from the smallest of things to the largest, emptiness graces us with sheer possibility, utility, and beauty.

Rilke once said being here is so much. Seeing, truly, arouses us to the joy and mystery of being. This is expressed wonderfully in a meditation from the Jesuit priest Anthony de Mello.[8] "What does it mean to be Enlightened?" a disciple once asked. "To see," the master replied. "To see what?" the disciple asked. "The hollowness of success, the emptiness of achievements, the nothingness of

6. Gen 2:2–3.

7. Lao Tzu, *Tao Te Ching*, 11.

8. De Mello, *Awakening*, 177.

human striving," said the master. The disciple was appalled. "But isn't that pessimism and despair?" "No," the master replied. "That's the excitement and freedom of the eagle gliding over a bottomless ravine."

8

THE UNGAME

In the 1980s, when my brother and I were still young, we used to play board games together as a family all the time. On the weekends we would play Clue or Sorry or Scrabble. If either of us got sick and had to stay home from school Monopoly was also a favorite pastime. We would even play games when we had guests over as an after-dinner activity.

I can recall one evening when my parents had invited the Fujita family over for dinner. They were a Japanese family my father had come to know through his work with Mr. Fujita at the University of Hartford. The Fujita children, of whom there were two, were always *so* well behaved. Not that my brother Dan and I weren't, just not on the same par I suppose. On this particular evening, prior to dessert and just after dinner, my parents announced that we were heading into the family room to play The Ungame. My brother and I were quietly elated. "A new game? This will be awesome!" we thought to ourselves as we exchanged smiles. (For those of you reading this whose homes might be inundated with video games, tablets, and the like, you have to keep in mind that, yes, believe it or not, board games were and still are a lot of fun.) Dan and I ran into the family room and proceeded to tear off the clear wrapping from the new game waiting there on the coffee table for us to play. We opened up the board, and set out a box full of questions. Dan and I asked our parents enthusiastically, "So how do we play?" My mother replied with a smile, "Oh, you'll see."

Mr. Fujita drew the first question. It was something like, "If you received five thousand dollars as a gift, how would you spend it?" We went around the room, allowing each person a chance to share how they would spend the five thousand dollars. Selfishly? Altruistically? Would they save it? Would they invest it? What would they get with it? Then, Mrs. Fujita drew the next card, which said something like, "What is your favorite thing to do in your spare time?" Again we went around the room giving everyone a chance to reflect and answer. The answers were wide and varied, and interesting to hear, but at this point my brother Dan and I were becoming a bit agitated. I looked at Dan like, "What kind of game *is* this?" So I asked my parents again, "How do we play this game? How do we know who's winning and who's losing? At least give us a clue." But my mother just smiled. "Let's keep playing," she said gently. "You'll see how it works." We drew another card with another question on it: "What are the three most important things in your life?" Then we drew another card: "What are you most afraid of?" And we drew another card: "What makes you angry?" At this point Dan and I were becoming angry. What the heck kind of game was this?

As it turns out, The Ungame is just that, a type of non-game with an emphasis on the absence of competition and, instead, the joy of reflection, conversation, and a deepening understanding of the other people in the "game." The Ungame is so-called because it's not a game about identifying who is the winner and who are the losers. It's not a game about pegging who was the smartest, and who wasn't, about who was physically superior, and who wasn't. It's not a game about making divisions to single out the best from the worst. It's not a game in any traditional sense of the word. I have to say I think Jesus would have very much liked The Ungame. The Jesus who rebuked his disciples when they began arguing about who was going to be greatest.[1] The Jesus who taught his followers not to judge.[2] The Jesus who placed an emphasis not on being *better* than others but on being a *servant* to others.[3]

Too often we see people making a game out of life, a competitive sport out of relationships. We tacitly compare ourselves to one another. We put others down in order to lift ourselves up. But self-worth so derived is the very definition of superficiality. There is no competition in love. Love seeks to honor the other, to befriend the other, to affirm the other. Love has enough depth in its own skin, and enough trust, not to worry about having a "one up" on another. In the kingdom of love there is simply no room for competition.[4] The beginning of love is the will to let those we love be perfectly themselves, without having to see them or ourselves as better or worse than the other, as Thomas Merton once pointed out.[5] The absence of the competitive eye can be liberating because there is no longer a preoccupation with appearances where one thing is judged as higher or lower, better or worse, in relation to me. The absence of the competitive spirit brings about levity in the soul where instead of looking for ways to criticize, evaluate, and judge we begin instead to look more for the good, the beautiful, and the blessed. To see these latter more than the former is truly a magnanimous gift in its own right.

I was a guest one morning not too long ago on San Diego Talk Radio and at one point in my conversation with the host I was asked, "So what is your church all about?" It was a no-brainer. I replied, simply and directly, "Love." Apparently, this very same one-word answer was an echo of what at least two other pastors had shared on the show earlier in the month, which was quite interesting and encouraging. Too often churches have been guilty of putting the Great Command and the so-called Great Commission on a par. But Jesus never called the latter great. Look it up. Loving

1. Luke 9:46–48.
2. Matt 7:1.
3. Luke 22:24–26.
4. O'Donohue, *Anam Cara*, 35–36.
5. Merton, *No Man Is an Island*, 177.

God, and loving people. This is the Christian faith in action at its very best. *Compassion*. This great command that Jesus taught as more important than anything else can become a mantra, in our minds and in our relationships, gradually washing away the hidden competitiveness and fear lurking beneath the surface in too many of us.

The need to win, to advance, to prove oneself better than another, according to early Chinese thought, is nothing less than a type of madness. The sage Chuang Tzu writes:

> When an archer is shooting for fun
> He has all his skill.
> If he shoots for a brass buckle
> He is already nervous.
> If he shoots for a prize of gold
> He goes blind
> Or sees two targets—
> He is out of his mind.
> His skill has not changed,
> But the prize divides him.
> He cares
> He thinks more of winning
> Than of shooting—
> And the need to win
> Drains him of power.[6]

There is no need to demonize baseball, soccer, and the like, wonderfully fun and entertaining sports. Indeed, teamwork in games and having a goal to work towards can be good things. There is no sense in denying that. Yet we need to be discerning of our motives in the course of everyday life where such competitive tendencies can set us at odds with another, even belittling others. Such tendencies are detrimental to the biblical way of encouraging one another and building one another up.[7]

A simple, constructive question to guide our everyday interactions would be: what am I leaving behind in the other? We

6. Merton, *The Way of Chuang Tzu*, 107.

7. 1 Thess 5:11.

all know there is no such thing as a raw experience. Every single moment is already infused with the trace of what the prior moments have left behind. Each "new" experience you have is riddled with the echo of what was said and done in the experiences immediately preceding it. Such echoes are a kind of absence. The something that was done to me in the past is no longer "there" (it is in the past now) yet it continues to bear an imprint on me, an impression, a trace. The "hello!" that I yell into a canyon reiterates itself in an echo and is caught up in a gradually fainting repetition tending towards extinction, never quite the same as the original "hello!" yet bearing a reflection of that original in the absence of that original. Today, what echo will the words you share with others leave behind? What trace will your actions leave behind? Heidegger, a philosopher, once said beautifully that we are custodians of deep and ancient thresholds.[8] Deep within you is a grace that longs to transcend the threshold of your being into the threshold of another, as a blessing, if you will allow it. Indeed, to allow such crossings of thresholds in our interactions with others is to bring about a more cruciform world filled with the delightful traces and eternal echoes of that which is sublime.

8. O'Donohue, *Anam Cara*, 42.

9

ZERO

Without zero so many of the great architectural and techno-logical feats throughout history and in our own day and age would be entirely impossible. Nothing—what zero signifies—quite literally has helped us along. But zero has a very personal dimension as well.

Have you ever felt empty? Most of us have. It's nothing to be ashamed of. It's a common experience in our journey through life. When we feel empty we often try to rationalize our way to a better mind-set or to fill the emptiness with *things*—purchases, distractions, temporary substitutions to replace what we're really searching for. Yet so often both the will to reason and the will to acquire fail to fill the emptiness inside us.

I can remember attending a Bible study one evening with Erin several years ago just before we were married. The pastor leading the study that night said something tremendous I've never forgotten: "The essence of grumbling and complaining is trying to find satisfaction in things that cannot satisfy." The words are so simple yet so true.

Things *cannot* satisfy. Not in any lasting way. Sure, we find fleeting pleasure in things, and we can enjoy that, and we should enjoy that, to some extent. But there is no real, permanent satisfaction in the things of this world. This inevitably creates torpor or, strangely enough, its opposite: restlessness. In the wake of our dissatisfactions we often either latch on to apathy or cling more likely in our day and age to incessant activity as an expression of our deep restlessness. Augustine said it best when he said our hearts are restless, until they rest in you, O God. But reason, too, not only our grasping after things, often falls short of filling the hole we sometimes sense in the midst of life. Our attempts to will ourselves past our emptiness, and to rationalize why we might ignore our intuition and sensibilities, ultimately only bring us back to the same spot from which we tried so ferociously to escape. A deeper kind of contentment begins to surface only as we zero out our over-estimation of the importance of the rational self and the acquisitional self. What we're truly looking for transcends.[1] It has less to do with logic, and things, and more to do with no-thing.

Chuang Tzu captures well this critical point in a wonderfully odd story:

> The Yellow Emperor went wandering
> To the north of the Red Water
> To the Kwan Lun mountain. He looked around
> Over the edge of the world. On the way home
> He lost his night-colored pearl.
> He sent out Science to seek his pearl, and got nothing.
> He sent Analysis to look for his pearl, and got nothing.
> He sent out Logic to seek his pearl, and got nothing.
> Then he asked Nothingness, and Nothingness had it!
> The Yellow Emperor said:
> "Strange, indeed: Nothingness
> Who was not sent
> Who did no work to find it
> Had the night-colored pearl!"[2]

It is interesting that in many ancient cultures the concept of nothingness of which Chuang Tzu speaks, that is the idea of zero,

1. Isa 55:2, 8–9.
2. Merton, *The Way of Chuang Tzu*, 74.

has had at times a rich and thoroughly positive association. In Central America, the Maya people used an attractive shell glyph as a zero symbol in their calendaring system. Zero in ancient Egyptian numeration, though absent as a placeholder, was present as a digit where the zero hieroglyph *nfr* had the corresponding meaning "beautiful." And in India the symbol for zero had associations with the majesty of space and sky.[3]

It is no accident that the nothingness of zero was associated with the beautiful in these ways. That humanity has been struck by zero in an aesthetic way says something profound about our enchantment with absence. Not only can the shape and content of things court the affections of the heart, but so too what is missing. Beauty has to do with more than just *things* and their forms. It has as much to do with the *lack* of things, the lack *in* things, that which lies *beyond* mere things. Beauty has to do with more than mere appearances. Not only substance but also absence has a lovely role to play in life.

Can you remember the last time you placed a zero on your calendar, instead of filling things *in* you purposefully took things *out*, leaving just one whole day blank? If not an entire day, can you recall the last time you zeroed out moments in your day? During an especially difficult time in my life, I was encouraged to do just this at the prompting of a spiritual mentor. My life had become full. It had become so full of so many wonderful things and yet it was almost as though that fullness had strangely led me to feel empty and in a way that haunted me at times for weeks on end. Then, I tried reclaiming moments, each day, where I would stop whatever I was doing for a little while. I would simply breathe. I would enjoy a short walk. I would do nothing, nothing more than perhaps listen to the breeze rustling the leaves in the branches of a large tree for a minute or two. These zero moments felt unmistakably odd at first. They felt like they were without any real purpose. Yet I was quietly surprised by the undeniable levity this zeroing immediately began to bring back into my life. I felt a gentle, caressing warmth returning to my inner life in these moments. Lightness.

3. Joseph, *The Crest of the Peacock*, 86.

Sometimes what we need most in life is homecoming. We need to come home to ourselves. We might think we are already at home in ourselves because we "are" ourselves and travel "with" ourselves everywhere we go. Yet we can be terribly far from ourselves. If we're not careful, it is all too easy to become out of touch with our inner life and with what really matters to us the most. Homecoming is a spiritual remedy of the highest order. It is important to remember that there are very few generalized principles for homecoming, however, for the art of being is as unique as you are. "The signature of this unique journey," writes John O'Donohue, "is inscribed deeply in each soul. If you attend to yourself and seek to come into your presence, you will find exactly the right rhythm for your own life."[4] Your very own self has the best map of where you need to go and what you need to be about. Zeroing out moments for being, breathing, *not* doing, can help to return you to yourself.

Nevertheless we must be cautious with zero and zeroing out moments in our lives. Absence can become a black hole that swallows us whole. Zero historically has also at times been viewed with great suspicion. Zero, that "O" without a figure, as Shakespeare called it, was associated in the Middle Ages with the void, most typically identified with evil. In alchemy, its shape appears as Ouroboros, the dragon swallowing its own tail, a shadowy, obstructive number.[5] Even the Maya people, it seems, had qualms with zero, for in addition to some of its symbol associations with beauty, they believed in nine Lords of the Night, gods of the underworld, who were ruled by the Death God, none other than (you guessed it) Zero himself.

Beautiful. Yet dangerous. Why such ambivalence about zero? We have a hard enough time dealing with the things of life. How much harder for us to make sense of the no-things in life! Perplexity surrounds the idea of absence at every turn. Anything with a name surely exists, and yet how can what "doesn't exist" (zero) exist? Is zero an actual number, or something more akin to a concept, like infinity, that's useful to the mathematical enterprise? As

4. O'Donohue, *Anam Cara*, 57–58.
5. Kaplan, *The Nothing That Is*, 187–89.

49

Robert Kaplan puts it in his book *The Nothing That Is: A Natural History of Zero*, "the disquieting question of whether zero is out there or a fiction will call up the perennial puzzle of whether we invent or discover the way of things . . . ."[6] Zero and what it signifies mystifies. As John Donne once said from his pulpit in 1620, "The less anything is, the less we know it: how invisible, how unintelligible a thing, then, is this *Nothing!*"[7]

Perhaps that is the point of zero and with zeroing out moments in our lives. We're not supposed to overdo it but we're also not supposed to "get it." The significance of nothing is not something that so easily lends itself to intellectual scrutiny. *Nothing* is not *something* that can be handled like the other things in life. Yet, when we practice it enough, we can almost immediately feel the difference. There is something mysterious and healing about just being. If instead of trying to *do* something with nothing, we allow moments for nothing, the rhythm of our soul can gradually become more apparent to us. There is space for that rhythm to appear, and for us to notice it. Who we are becomes clearer. Truly, the beauty and brilliance in each of our lives then shines all the brighter.

6. Ibid., 20.

7. Ibid., 192–93.

10

THE GIFT OF DEATH

I received a phone call the other day. My old friend Nathan on the other end of the line shared with me the news that our friend Jamie had taken his life. I didn't know how to respond or what to say. Despite my training in pastoral care and grief ministry, I felt caught off guard suddenly receiving such news about someone whom I had been so close to for a time. The announcement felt unmistakably intimate. It reminded me of how cautiously and tenderly we must tread when upon the shores of another's loss. It is always one thing to know *of* a passing, or to be a comforting presence in the midst of *another* person's experience of the absence of a loved one. It is quite another thing to feel that loss personally and palpably yourself. "How terrible the absence of our beloved dead, and how beautiful their continued presence in memory," observes Kathleen Norris.[1] Yet even the space, in between such presence and absence, the space that marks the knowledge of that transition, that space, too, is ripe with mystery and a contradiction of forces and feelings.

I had known Jamie during our middle school and high school years. He was a tall guy, even at our young age, towering above his

1. Norris, *Acedia & me*, 250.

peers at around six feet two inches. His height, it seemed, was a gift from his father who had come from England and who both stood and spoke majestically, like a king. Jamie and I would often hang out after school, finding the ability to laugh together about the most ridiculous topics the easiest thing in the world to do. We took jujitsu classes together, and during the droll of the summer months we took to making short films with my parents' video camera—usually horror flicks filled with the ample use of Karo syrup comingled with red food coloring for the effect of blood. Receiving the news of Jamie's suicide, and the particular way he chose to go by hanging himself, was not horrific though. It was something else. It was numbing. I finally managed to speak to Nathan through the telephone the only honest words I could find: "Jamie? Really? *Really?*" I said in disbelief. "I'm so sorry . . . ." There was no profundity to be shared here. Sometimes the absence of many words and the simplicity of a shared sigh is more than enough.

When someone we care about dies and suddenly we experience the absence of that person, whose presence was so richly felt in our lives for a time, the significance of absence—even though it is a nothingness, the lack of presence—is nevertheless felt deeply. Absence has it's own kind of weight. Suicide is particularly weighty because of what it is. It is not the accidental or timely moving of one's presence into the absence that is death. It is absence chosen, and with an unmistakable finality about it. What Shakespeare poetically phrased as a question "to be or not to be" suicide answers, shockingly, "*not* to be." What Albert Camus called *the* philosophical question—the choice to live, after one has received the gift of life without any choice in the matter whatsoever—is a question suicide answers in the negative. The reason for suicide is said most typically to be the need for escape—escape from what is perceived to be irresolvable emotional or relational distress. Yet this reason surely cannot encompass the totality of the mystery that lies behind such an ultimate choice. I know something of this personally. I was never outright suicidal myself. Still, I can remember during my late teenage years climbing a fire escape ladder one night to the top of the local florist building where I worked and sitting crouched near the ledge, peering down at the lights of the town below and wondering during a season of personal darkness and self-transformation the eternal question, "Why?"

Notwithstanding the darkness of suicide, it is ironic that so much of the luminosity of spiritual insight, even across cultural divides, has emphasized the need, in a sense, to go the route of suicide, to choose death. Not in the way my dear friend Jamie chose death, God rest his soul, but to choose death in a slightly different way, a way that actually heightens and illuminates life: embracing the reality of death, in *this* life, as a path to knowing the abundance of life.

"Thanatologists" of various types (doctors, pastors, and the like) know this all too well. By virtue of working closely with those on the precipice of death, they have come to see all too clearly that avoiding or ignoring the reality of death is beyond foolishness. It is psychically damaging. Acknowledging death, facing death, talking about our mortality, the fading of the self, the immanence of absence—these are the things that open us to the possibility of real living in the here and now.

Jesus himself alludes to this when he says, "Don't run from suffering; embrace it."[2] He comes even more directly to the point when he says, "Whoever wants to save their life will lose it, but whoever loses their life for me and for the gospel will save it."[3] He says elsewhere, similarly, "Whoever finds their life will lose it, and whoever loses their life for my sake will find it"[4] and "whoever wants to save their life will lose it, but whoever loses their life for me will find it."[5] What Jesus is getting at here is something we cannot afford to miss. Jesus wants us to see something very difficult for most of us to see, at least initially. To borrow the words of Jacques Derrida, death is a gift.[6] It is only when we die to ourselves—our own desires, plans, and ambitions—that we then really

2. Mark 8:34.

3. Mark 8:35.

4. Matt 10:39.

5. Matt 16:25.

6. Derrida, *The Gift of Death*, 36–53.

begin to experience life. We must lay it all down, our entire lives, first, before we begin to taste the amazing and wild abundance that is life. Yes, we begin to experience life *biologically* from the moment we are born, what the Bible terms *bios* life. But *true* life, *real* living, what the Bible terms *zoe* life, life not apart from but rather immersed in communion with God, that kind of life doesn't happen by accident. It takes a radical shift in one's life, a paradigm shift, nothing less than total surrender, the death of the self, the absenting of the self, which makes room for the beauty and abundance of God.

Christian wisdom famously states this essential movement from death to life in the following maxim from Jesus: deny yourself, take up your cross, and follow me.[7] The Reformation theologian John Calvin believed these simple words formed the very essence and epitome of the entire Christian journey, indeed, the essence and epitome of the human journey, a path from death to life and not the other way around.[8] Take a moment to slow down and read Jesus' instruction to us again. Notice what his words so vividly describe. Following the One does not essentially mean affirming but rather *denying* the self, *absenting* the self. Following Jesus does not mean choosing life, not in the first instance, but rather first choosing the cross, the Roman symbol of death, disgrace, and humiliation. Yet the fascinating power to which the Christian life attests is that the acceptance and embrace of death, in truth, is a gift that leads to the fullness of life. We begin to experience real life when life is about something More than *me, me, me*. Herein lies the paradoxical nature of the cross, the central symbol of Christian faith, no longer a symbol of death, or at least only death, but now a symbol of resurrection and the gift of new life.

We hear traces of this truth about the gift of death in other places as well. Lao Tzu, for example, says this: "Allow yourself to yield, and you can stay centered. Allow yourself to bend, and you will stay straight. Allow yourself to be empty, and you'll get

---

7. Luke 9:23.

8. Calvin, *Institutes of the Christian Religion*, 689–701.

filled up. Allow yourself to be exhausted, and you'll be renewed."[9] Within the milieu of ancient Chinese thought out of which Lao Tzu writes, we have to remember there are two principle forces in the universe, referred to as yin and yang. Yang is associated with light, life, power, and presence. Yin is associated with the opposite, namely, darkness, death, yielding, absence. When Lao Tzu says, "allow yourself to be empty, and you'll get filled up" he is saying that yin leads to yang and not the other way around. Emptiness is primary. Emptying is essential. Allowing yourself to yield, even to move toward a kind of exhaustion, to move toward depletion, indeed, a kind of death, absence, and emptiness, this is the Way of bringing yourself into oneness with the originating and overarching force of the universe, Tao. Death is not an end but a gateway.

The Celtic wisdom of John O'Donohue likewise reminds us to see that death is a horizon and a pervasive one at that: "We are wrong to think that death comes only at the end of life."[10] In truth, death in this life, which is a moving into absence, suffuses our experience. This kind of death, where things in our lives continually leave us, frightens us such that we often feel tempted and even desperate to fill the emptiness. "We are haunted with a deep sense of absence. There is something missing from our lives. We always expect it to be filled by a definite person, object, or project. We are desperate to fill this emptiness, but the soul tells us, if we listen to it, that this absence can never be filled."[11] Deep down we know this. Better, therefore, that we work towards accepting absence as much as we do the gift of presence. Absence is as much a part of life as presence, and the wise learn to embrace both.

The gift of death can strike us as paradoxical and perplexing and rightly it should. For here we are approaching Mystery, using words to describe something that very much resists the container of words and, instead, desires to be experienced, inasmuch as one can experience "death" in this life before the literal death that awaits us. Denying yourself. Emptying yourself. Embracing

9. Lao Tzu, *The Tao Te Ching of Lao Tzu*, 22.

10. O'Donohue, *Anam Cara*, 199.

11. Ibid., 222.

absence. These are all ways of encouraging us to really live life. To do that requires the gift of death, letting go of self, strivings, holding on too tightly to our own plans and agendas, which always seem to have a way of slipping through our fingers anyway. Accepting absence in life is never easy. It is usually painful. It is a process, and not one unlike the Christian image of resurrection, where letting go must precede our rising up, like being birthed into existence all over again.[12] Death frightens us, perhaps more so than anything, because it is a nothing, not even an experience to be had alongside other experiences in life, as Ludwig Wittgenstein so aptly put it, because death is the very cessation and absence of experience itself.[13] Yet before that physical death becomes us, we *must* open ourselves to experiencing this *other* kind of death that is critical for us to experience—and that so again and again and again—allowing unnecessary things to fade from our lives so that we might make more room for life, participating in what I would call "cyclic soteriology" for those theologically inclined readers who find treasures in terminology.[14]

What in your life are you holding on to too tightly? Where would you do well to yield? What do you need to let go? Allowing your self to experience the difficulty and even humiliation that might go hand-in-hand with an honest, personal probing of such questions can be a great blessing.[15] There is virtue in emptying yourself, of your self, so that you might have the greater capacity to embody Life. Death in this way is a gift.

12. John 3:1–17.

13. Death is the absence of life and therefore we do not live to experience death. "Death is not an event of life." Wittgenstein, *Tractatus Logico-Philosophicus*, 116.

14. We change *repeatedly* in our journey with the sacred rather than once for all; *metanoia* is multifarious.

15. Prov 18:12.

11

ABSENCE MAKES THE HEART GROW FONDER

I recently traveled to New York via US Airways on a redeye flight that happened to be scheduled on the night of a blue moon. The view outside the tiny window next to my seat was breathtaking. I was reminded of lovely words from the Dhammapada: "Like the moon, come out from behind the clouds! Shine."[1]

Moonlight graced the soft clouds moving gently below that danced with lightning illuminating an otherwise dark and spacious sky. Yet there in the midst of the sublime no sooner was I traveling away from home than I was missing it. Painfully so. Strikingly so. I was missing my wife Erin whose very thought made me misty-eyed at the airport terminal. My admiration and adoration for her words cannot express. Barely more than an hour had passed since I had seen my beautiful daughter face-to-face, or my son who is so sweet. But already I was feeling a vacancy in my heart that hurt. *Heartache*. A sinking feeling in my center. A reminder of how much it hurts to be human, even apart from life's toils, traps, disappointments, and disasters. Distance is one of the lonely aspects of space.[2] Absence, from things, and especially the

1. Gautama Buddha, *Dhammapada*, 25:23.
2. O'Donohue, *Four Elements*, 8.

people we love, is one of the most powerful forces we feel if we feel anything deeply in this life at all. I enjoyed my trip to New York. Still, the return home was sweeter. There is much to be said for the old adage absence makes the heart grow fonder.

Absence in our relationships can be a true gift. To be away from those we love for a time hurts. But it hurts in a good way, not only negatively. It is also a positive pain. The pain would not be there had it not been for the love. The pain is an aching, yes, yet one filled with the potent reminder of who and what and why we love. The pain is also a reminder of the joyful anticipation of reuniting. This is true of those we long to see again in this life and in the life to come. We may or may not choose such absence from those we love. The absence may be an appropriate respite from those we normally see day-to-day or the absence may be violently forced upon us by the hazards of living in this precarious world of ours. When absence comes our way, however it comes, we must remember that the empty feeling of absence has in faith, beyond only pain, a sweet promise attached to it. Jesus promised for the life to come, "In my Father's house are many rooms; if it were not so, I would have told you. I am going there to prepare a place for you. And if I go and prepare a place for you, I will come back and take you to be with me that you also may be where I am."[3] His promise is a promise of happy union and reunion, a homecoming that fills and overwhelms the heart with delight. In this life, too, we can be attentive to the absences that make the heart grow fonder. Indeed, we should be attentive to these absences because they have so very much to teach us—especially those absences in which we find ourselves far from God.

Erin and the kids arrived home after swimming at the pool the other day with a story to share. After Bella and Josh went to their bedrooms to change, Erin told me how a couple of the other children had been giving Josh a hard time, for no good reason, other than that kids will be kids. As she explained the details of what transpired I felt so proud of my son. Erin told of how he simply shrugged the annoyance off, like it was nothing, and resisted

3. John 14:2–3.

responding in kind. Hearing this significantly diluted any anger I would have otherwise felt. Joshua, like his big sister, is larger than life—always has been—as demonstrated by the wonderfully large smile he typically wears, cheek to cheek, with the purest of joy coming through in his countenance. He rises above. As a father, still, I couldn't help but feel a bit heavy-hearted over the whole thing. When we or those we love are scathed by the unkindness of others, and when we ourselves perpetrate such unkindness, even in the seemingly smallest of forms, we either feel, or create, distance between us and God.

As Erin had been sharing the details of the afternoon and Josh's admirable response, I found my mind unexpectedly wandering back to my own childhood. Not to any kind of similar moments of nobility. Just the opposite in fact. I suddenly remembered something that hadn't crossed my mind in decades, as if some synapses in my brain were suddenly making a connection once again that had been lost in the dark matter of my mind. It was a parent-teacher conference night at my elementary school, or was it an open house? It was something like that, and we kids were all out on the playground while the adults were inside cycling through the classrooms. When the playground supervisors weren't looking, I spotted another kid I didn't like and decided to do something about him. I'm not sure why I didn't like him. He had never done anything wrong to me. I had somehow simply decided one day that I didn't like him very much. So, I convinced two of my friends to hold him for a second while I kicked him in the groin. I am deeply ashamed of this. Acknowledging this incident, this sin, feels like I'm telling a tale of someone else's life. Yet it is part of my own story. I see now (though I did not see it at the time) that in that moment I was not only absenting myself of my own humanity through unprovoked violence toward another. More than that, I was far from God.

The Bible is replete with instances of such distance between humanity and God. The experience of the absence of the presence of God at times comes about through sin when humanity turns away from God. Sometimes the absence is mysterious as in the book of Esther where "God" is not mentioned even once and we're not entirely sure why. At other times, it is pain, loss, and sometimes it is even God's own doing that creates the space.

The face of God turns away from Moses, on purpose, because it is too much glory, too much splendor, too much radiance, it is simply *too much* for Moses to bear.[4] It is God's choice to create some distance there, absenting Godself in form for Moses' own good. Absence. For his own good. Now that's worth pondering.

Doesn't Jesus teach us the same? In his farewell address Jesus says to his disciples, "It is for your own good that I am going away. Unless I go away, the Advocate will not come to you. . . . But when he, the Spirit of truth, comes, he will guide you into all the truth."[5] This sounds strange to our ears at first living in a culture and social climate that places a great and positive emphasis on presence. We like to erase space, to erase the time it takes to hyperlink from one web page to another, to travel from one destination to another, from one activity to the next, incessantly trying to squeeze more and more in all the while forcing space out. Presence is very meaningful, to be sure, but it is not the whole picture. Jesus reminds his disciples of this here. It is not only the coming of the Christ that is a blessing, he says, but also the leaving. It is not only the presence of the Christ that is a gift, but also the absence of the Christ. There is a necessary relationship, a continuous interplay between presence and absence. Indeed, as Henri Nouwen points out, the great mystery of the divine revelation in Christ is that God entered into intimacy with us not only by Christ's coming, but also by his leaving.[6] Without the absence of the Christ, Jesus says, there would not be room for the Spirit of truth to guide his beloved into "all the truth." Entering into the fullness of truth requires not only the gift of presence, but also of absence.

We see how far this is from a theoretical idea when we look at the lives of people like Alfred Delp, Corrie ten Boom, and Dietrich Bonhoeffer, who, while in Nazi prison camps awaiting death,

4. Exod 33:18–23.
5. John 16:7, 13.
6. Nouwen, *The Living Reminder*, 42–43.

experienced Christ's presence in the midst of his absence.[7] In one of his letters Bonhoeffer writes: "The God who is with us is the God who forsakes us (Mark 15:34) . . . Before God and with God we live without God."[8]

After escaping from slavery in Egypt, the Hebrew people experience the gift of absence. All too quickly they forget the graciousness of the God who frees them, they get lost in the wilderness for forty years and endure a prolonged period of by-and-large the experience of the absence of the presence of God in their lives. Yet it is during this time of being (or is it just feeling?) far away from God that they learn something invaluable, something they perhaps could not have learned in any other way as powerfully had they not had that period of absence, an absence in which their hearts grow fonder once again for the divine presence. They learn that there is truly *nobody* else like God. No *thing* matters more. No *one* matters more. God *is* all in all, and that is no mere doctrine to commit to memory. It is truth, truth that totally transforms your life. Not only the presence of God, but God's absence, reveals this to them.

Similarly, when I am away from my wife and children their preciousness is revealed to me in a new way. I find I am able to articulate my love for Bella and Josh, as I am doing here in this meditation, with novelty and clarity. I am able to understand and appreciate more deeply how much Erin and I have to celebrate in each other. The distance actually affords me some perspective. When I am far from them, I see them, I see them in a new light, a gift that seems to go in tandem with the heartache of missing them.

When we feel far from God, the heart aches in a deep way, like nothing else. We may feel far from God because we have been up to our old tricks again, acting more like Cain than Able. We may feel as though God is absent for a time because we are hurting for any number of reasons. Living is the promise of pain. Jesus says to his followers, "In this world you will have trouble . . . ." I love

7. Ibid., 42.

8. Bonhoeffer, *Letters and Papers from Prison*, 360.

how much of a realist Jesus is about our state of affairs. He adds this, however, to complete the realism: "But take heart, for I have overcome the world."[9]

In this world of trouble, absence is very much a reality, yet one that does make the heart grow fonder. Fonder of what we truly long for, and fonder of what we really need. Relationships that matter. People who mean the world to us. God. If we are destined to deal with some absence from such blessings in this life, then let us remember that this absence can be more than just heartache. Absence is a spaciousness that helps the heart to grow.

9. John 16:33.

12

SILENCE

Back in the 1950s there was an American composer by the name of John Cage who walked onto a stage one evening before a full audience to perform his new composition entitled *4' 33"* (pronounced "four minutes, thirty-three seconds"). He bowed before the gracious audience, sat down at his piano, gingerly raised his fingers to play, and then began—by *not* playing. Cage the avant-garde began his piece and continued his piece right up to the end by not playing a single note for the duration of four minutes and thirty-three seconds. At the conclusion of his performance, he stood up, took a bow, and quietly walked off the stage.

What I love about John Cage is not only his eccentricity but his insight. Music, in truth, is as much about the absence of sound as it is about the presence of sound. Without the separation in between the notes—the space—a song could not be a song, or at least not a very good song. It would be mere noise, the constant uninterrupted continuity of sound. Cage noticed this and did something to articulate the gravity of this point. He created an entire musical piece devoted to absence, thus redefining song as such in the process.

I cannot help but think that the steps leading to this entirely creative composition were somehow rooted in the Spirit. At the threshold of the human and the sublime there lies a lovely originality and spontaneity. In the liminality of creativity there is something sacred that makes the heart dance in new ways. At the precipice of the void we find the expression of truth and our truest selves. The void that 4' 33" embodies hints at this truth. It is the truth of the power and near omnipresence of silence.

It is interesting that some of the most significant realities there are marking this universe of ours are characterized by silence. Time, like a river, as Einstein imagined, flows through us and around us on every side without exception, constantly moving us down stream from one point to another without our say in the matter whatsoever. Yet, all the while, this powerful and all-encompassing force does so silently.

Space, too, engulfs us, indeed *is* the very fabric of our universe along with time. Without space, there is no place for us, or anything at all, to be. Here on this planet, minuscule within the utterly unimaginable vastness that is the universe, we have air and molecules that allow for sound vibrations to travel, and thus we have sound and noise. But within most of the universe, which is space, space beyond space and more space for trillions upon trillions of light years and more, there is nothing but absolute silence. . . . There is an eerie quality to the silence of time and space. As Ridley Scott aptly put it in his science fiction thriller *Alien*: "No one can hear you scream in space." What a great line.

Even God, who does speak to us at times in that still small voice with words of love, encouragement, and guidance along the way, nevertheless, for so many is so often the One who abides with us *less* in words and *more* in the sweetness of silence. "Silence is God's first language; everything else is a poor translation" Thomas Keating once said.[1] When the prophet Zephaniah commands the people to "be silent before the Sovereign Lord"[2] one has to wonder if this is not only to get us to listen more to God, but also

1. Keating, *Invitation to Love*, 105.

2. Zeph 1:7.

as much to mirror the way of God. After all, Scripture does teach us to be imitators of God.[3]

Time. Space. God. That silence marks some of the most significant realities there are in this universe of ours tells us that there is something profoundly significant about silence itself. There is something for us to learn from silence, something important for us to pay attention to in silence.

Why is it, then, that so often we avoid silence? We cringe at any "awkward silence" when talking with others. We do our best to fill so much of our time with noise of various kinds: listening to the radio in the car, our iPods when we walk or run, having the television on at home, even if we're not watching it, constantly filling the voids in our conversations with talk even about the most inane topics. Conversation is a gift but not ubiquitously necessary. One of the things I love about the time I have with my wife Erin on the weekends is the uncommon ability we have to simply sit and be with each another. Yes, we talk plenty, too, and that time is very good. But we also enjoy just *being*, with each other, no words necessary. Like honey there is something extremely sweet about shared silence with those we love. There is a gift that we give each other there in the absence of our words as much as in the sharing of our words. The absence of a perceived need for incessant conversation creates space for a deeper kind of presence, presence to each other, and presence with each other.

A few years back I went on a solo retreat in the Pocono Mountains. Food and a mattress on the floor were provided in a rustic cabin with one rule for the duration of my stay: no talking. If you were walking outside from one part of the retreat center to another and happened to pass another person, you should do nothing more than smile, I was told. If you were eating breakfast in one of the communal kitchens and another happened to wander in for breakfast, you could enjoy one another's company, as long as you did so without words. Here, for a few days, time and space were intentionally carved out for honoring the gift and power of silence.

3. Eph 5:1.

I have to say that even for someone such as myself who is more readily inclined towards silence and solitude, I found the experience at first both inviting and strange. Yet, as I persevered, there was something alluring, simple, and good about the silence that ministered to me. Saint Isaac of Nineveh got it right when he said, "In the beginning we have to force ourselves to be silent. But then, from our very silence is born something that draws us into deeper silence."[4]

As I went deeper, hour after hour, day after day, I noticed something while submerged in the silence. I noticed, first, how much self-talk I have (we have) constantly going on inside. There is an internal voice running almost constantly and often without our even being aware of it. My self-talk was at times rather blasé, at other times marked by gratitude, joy, and anticipation, and at other times downright critical and negative. I also noticed, secondly, a sense of release that gradually swept over me. Beyond what words can say, it felt *good* to be in the silence (after I got past the transition). It felt wonderful. When Jesus taught his disciples that you will know the truth and the truth will set you free,[5] I think he must have had in mind not only the truth of God but also the truth of ourselves which is rooted in God, something silence brings us face to face with.

We often fear facing ourselves. It is common to busy ourselves in order to avoid any real time with ourselves. If it is a fearful thing to fall into the hands of the living God,[6] because truth is often like a shock and awe campaign on the soul, then so too can it be a fearful thing to simply be with the truth of one's self. That is because too often we live in ways that diverge from the truth of ourselves. We are divergent. We fear the memory of difficult things that have happened to us. We fear the guilt and shame that might arise if we spend too much time looking in the mirror of the self. We fear the emptiness we might feel in our silence and solitude, and the deep penetrating questions that may arise. Jesus, aware of our fears, but

4. De Mello, *Awakening*, 370.
5. John 8:32.
6. Heb 10:31.

also of the deeper and liberating power of truth, lovingly told his followers on more than one occasion not to be afraid.[7] We need to face the truth of ourselves, and more than that we need to learn to be with the truth of ourselves, our great possibilities, and also our real limitations, because the alternative is living a lie. Fear unchecked distorts and misshapes our true identity and destiny in life.

Our fears take other forms as well. When another person is grieving the loss of a loved one, sometimes we fear not knowing what to do or say. In the Old Testament we hear about how Job's three friends experience this. They slip into the error of trying to *explain* Job's suffering in the wake of the death of his children, and having lost most other things dear to him as well. They suggest to Job crass things like, "It's only because you're so holy that God has deemed you worthy to endure such a trial" and "It's your sin that brought you misfortune because God is just and only deals each of us what we deserve." Not surprisingly Job does not find these words very comforting. If anything, their words only serve to intensify his pain. However, there is something helpful that Job's three friends do for him just prior to all their mangled words. The very first thing they do, when they come to visit Job in his grief, is to sit down with him and say nothing.[8] For seven days and seven nights they simply sit with Job in silence. They give Job the gift of their presence, absent of words, and minus the broken logic that always tries but fails to make sense of why bad things happen in a world created by a good God. This is their best gift to Job.

I once heard John O'Donohue say in an interview that what we need most desperately today is a pedagogy of interiority. I couldn't agree more. Going within and carving out regular time for silence in our lives is vital to the human spirit. It doesn't matter your personality type. The need to be acquainted with the truth of your self, which is rooted in the truth of God, is a universal one. Whatever we might fear encountering in silence the truth is that it is a great gift because there is so much more beyond fear in

7. Matt 10:36, 14:27; Mark 4:39–40, 5:36.
8. Job 2:11–13.

silence. There is God. Paul taught, "You are temples of the Holy Spirit."[9] Jesus believed, "The kingdom of God is within you."[10] Rumi said, "When I am silent, I have thunder hidden inside."[11] Rilke said, "Nobody can advise you and help you, nobody. There is only one way. Go into yourself."[12] The teachings go on, but let us not overuse them for there is already a tremendous contradiction and irony in my words here in presuming to talk about silence and the silent interior. The point is clear. There is a gift awaiting us in the silence. What we truly need and yearn for is not far, not outside ourselves, in another, or in a book, this book or any other. The gift is close. We simply need to have faith in the proximity of the gift God has placed within our hearts. Jesus, early in the morning, made a habit of going off for a little while to enjoy some silence and solitude before beginning his day.[13] What a phenomenal example.

9. 1 Cor 3:16. ,
10. Luke 17:21.
11. Rumi, *1,001 Pearls of Spiritual Wisdom*, 189.
12. Rilke, *Letters to a Young Poet*, 7.
13. Mark 1:35; Luke 5:16.

13

THE MOST SIGNIFICANT CHAPTER

14

AN EXPLANATION OF THE MOST
SIGNIFICANT CHAPTER

The great irony of this book has no doubt already occurred to you. Writing a book (something) about nothing is an inherent contradiction and a delightful one at that. Yet, lest you think I'm only joking about the title of the previous chapter, which I am quite serious about (though not too serious), allow me to offer an explanation for why in my estimation of things it truly is the most significant chapter in this book.

Why is it that when we read a text we primarily pay attention to the presumed content, that is, the words? I take this to be the case not only because we are trained to read this way from the time we are children but also because as a matter of habit we are visually trained to look for "somethings" in life as more important than "nothings." But we presume too much here. No one is denying that the word content of a book matters. Clearly it does matter. Yet if it were not for the margins surrounding the pages in our books, the empty spaces that mark *this* page in *this* book, and the spaces in between *all* the words and the letters of the chapters that comprise any book, texts would be unintelligible. A book would be an amusing run-on blanket of letters, a hodgepodge indecipherable and practically useless. What I'm getting at is the fact that nothing *counts* just as much as something, providing likewise absolutely essential content, in the written word and even beyond the horizon of the text. Knowing this opens our vision to begin seeing life in a wonderfully different way, to appreciate the light *and* the shadows, the gift of presence but also the gift of absence.

In truth the significance of the previous chapter really doesn't require much explanation at all. It is clear. In a book about nothing, such as this, of course the most important chapter would be and should be ripe with nothing! I've had great fun over the past year in telling those who have asked me how my book on nothing was coming along that I have spent long hours in front of a blank computer screen, poised to type, but not typing anything at all. Depending on the person, some laugh while others raise an eyebrow or clear their throats. But absence does warrant our attention, if for no other reason than there is so much of it. It's there in our books, in our homes, in the world, and in our lives making a difference. The abundance of absence we might say shows us that absence is full of tender presence, impressing upon us in so many different ways an eternal blessing for those ready to acknowledge it, for we could not be without the space to be.

Space is something we tend to notice when we move from a little to a lot of it and vice versa. I was attending an international martial arts seminar one summer in Boston where the room being used for our workouts was about half the size of the room we had used the previous year. A friend said to me as he looked around the room upon entering how it seemed like a smaller turnout this year. It actually wasn't. It was an illusion. The attendance was the same. It only appeared there were fewer people because there was less space. It is interesting how sometimes the opposite can create the same illusion, depending on one's perspective, where more space gives one the sense of fewer people compared to a smaller space. Either way, when space shifts we notice. When emptiness decreases or increases, our eyes adjust and our attention follows. This is important to understand not only about physical space but also in terms of the space we allow or don't allow in our day-to-day lives: space for communing with God, space for rest and rejuvenation in a fast-paced hyperlinking world, space for family and friends. When we take time and space to slowdown on a vacation, for example, we may become aware of bad habits we have allowed to creep in, draining us of life.

The previous chapter might be thought of in terms of content and context. Content and context define one another. They make each other meaningful. We need to remember as Robert Kaplan points out "that when each is pared to a minimum, a dab of one intensifies the other—and a context of nothing at all pins everything on the minutest presence. An empty presence, turn for turn, must bring the context into focus . . . ."[1] In dying congregations, for example, sometimes a more dynamic pastoral presence is called for in order to turn around the negative context. In thriving congregations, however, with a history of healthy habits and the right leaders plugged into the right spots, an empty and more invisible individual to love the already blessed congregation is all that's needed. Pastoral invisibility in such churches allows the already strong congregational context to shine in its own right. This principle can be applied to many different kinds of environments and relationships.

What is the content and context of the previous chapter? The content is nothing. But notice how the nothing of the previous chapter is not the same as the nothing, say, surrounding you this very moment in the room where you are reading this. The context defines the content. The context, here, is a book. When you stumbled upon the previous chapter and its empty pages, the nothingness there was surely encountered differently than if you had just walked into a room devoid of any furniture. In others words, emptiness *is* something we interact with and that so in a great variety of ways because of how content and context profoundly shape one another. So, what impression did the nothingness of the previous chapter make upon you? Did you smile and quickly move on? Did you stop to take "it" all in? Did you muse over the meaning

1. Kaplan, *The Nothing That Is*, 199.

or maybe more so the feeling of nothingness there? The context of the previous chapter—the fact that this is a book—indicates there is something there to be read. We simply need to "read" it in a way different from how we read the traditional content of a chapter, the words. What I would suggest might be most interesting, if you were to return to "read" the previous chapter, is to notice what the chapter draws out of you as opposed to what chapters typically do, that is, put something into us.

If you glossed over the previous chapter I encourage you to go back. Spend just a minute on each of the three blank pages, a trinity of minutes, doing nothing. Being. Breathing. Enjoying the most significant chapter in this book.

15

WOUNDOLOGY

E xperience wounds us. To live is to be bruised. Our inner wounds cry out for healing. Yet they need the right kind of attention, a certain kind of compassion. With our wounds we tend to gravitate toward one of two extremes.[1] We sometimes revisit the battered and hurt areas within us in an analysis-driven way, trying to make sense of the suffering, going back to a wound and opening it up again and again. We take off the protective healing skin that has formed around the wound, making it sore, making it weep again. This is an intrusive way of bringing attention to our wounds. If we skip this route, however, too often we go to another extreme where we completely avoid our wounds. This approach feels easier, at first, but ultimately fails us, as the pain settles into the soil of the soul. The truth about our wounds (as much as we might wish this were not the case) is that our wounds grow us. Nietzsche got it right when he said that which doesn't kill you makes you stronger. Yet when we attend to our wounds, we need to do so less analytically and more tenderly. You should not blame others or yourself for mistakes that you deeply regret. Sometimes you have grown through these mistakes. They

1. O'Donohue, *Anam Cara*, 181–83.

have brought you unexpectedly to a place you otherwise would not have arrived at. We ought to bring a compassionate mindfulness to the mistakes and wounds of our lives. The overly analytical only wounds further. Yet abandoning our wounds likewise leaves us at a loss. We need to treat these areas, but with great tenderness. "Areas of inner neglect and abandonment cry out to you,"[2] observes John O'Donohue. They want and need our attention. The wounds we too often absent ourselves from are very often some of the most vital areas of our lives.

I was writing these very words one afternoon when abruptly the writing was taken away because of a wound. Time I thought I had for reflection was replaced suddenly by a sharp, shooting pain in my upper abdomen. I tried to ignore the discomfort at first, hoping it would pass. But as the minutes ticked on by it became increasingly difficult to think a single thought. Pain does that, tearing at our most basic functionalities. Whether it's the wounding of physical pain, or spiritual and emotional pain, it is interesting that one of the first things to go is our ability and tendency to rationalize. Pain and suffering seem to smirk at our attempts to explain, negotiate, and compartmentalize the dark asymmetries of life.

As the pain continued to intensify, my writing came to a halt and I wondered what to do about the evening worship service I was scheduled to lead in an hour and a half. The service is a lovely new venture at our church, only a few years old with a humble, faithful following of forty individuals, worshippers whom I dare say probably would not be in the church at all if not for this more contemplative worship experience characterized by low lighting, communion, prayer, candle lighting, and passionate melodies that can easily bring healing tears to the eyes. Fortunately, I just happened to have another pastor assisting me with the service that evening, so I delegated my responsibilities to him and then quickly drove to the nearest hospital.

By the time I arrived just thirty minutes later my pain had doubled. I could barely get myself in the front door. Once I did, I learned there was at least a twenty-five minute wait until a doctor

2. Ibid., 181.

could see me. So, I did the only thing I could do. I waited. I sat there in the waiting room, waiting, and waiting some more, eyes closed in gripping pain, trying my best not to think about it, to distract myself from the pain, to remember pertinent Bible passages to ease my pain—anything and everything that might bring some relief. This is what we do in the midst of pain: we try our best to turn away from it.

Once the doctor was finally able to see me, I was given a shot of morphine and promptly wheeled over to the emergency room. My wound, the doctors discovered, was an upper abdominal hematoma. Feeling a bit foolish, I learned that it was caused by exercising too hard of all things, a wound that could have easily been prevented. But rather than beating myself up over the mistake that night—or for the next week as I was more or less bedridden—I found my mind wandering, naturally being drawn to look beyond only my physical wound and toward some other *inner* wounds, wounds I had been avoiding, and didn't even realize.

The hematoma had given me a week of forced absence: downtime for my body, but also for my soul, to heal. What I was able to work through internally and privately that week was crucial. The wounding turned out to be such a gift.

I am thankful for the wound, in retrospect. If I could go back to erase this painful bit of my history, honestly, I would not. What the wound essentially did was leave me with the gift of space. My writing for the afternoon was taken away. My work and meetings for the week were taken away. What remained (whether I liked it or not) was emptiness.

Sometimes we need emptiness. Sometimes we need things taken away. The Bible reminds us, "the Lord gives and the Lord takes away."[3] This is such a well-known passage, and with good reason. *Constantly* things are being given, and taken away, in life. There is a rhythm of presence *and* absence to our experience. This Bible verse contains words spoken to God from Job after he's dealt a crushing blow by Satan (or is it a crushing blow dealt to Job indirectly by God? It's really hard to tell when you read that opening

3. Job 1:21.

chapter of the book of Job). I like the ERV translation of this passage the best: "When I was born into this world, I was naked and had nothing. When I die and leave this world, I will be naked and have nothing. The Lord gives, and the Lord takes away. Praise the name of the Lord!"[4]

It's true: we arrive upon the stage of our lives with nothing, and we leave in the same way, with nothing. Nothing marks our beginning and our end. Things we acquire along the way—lest we forget—are temporary holdings of ours. Our children are never to be held too tightly. They are born as the sons and daughters of Life's longing for itself.[5] They are not ours. They, too, will be taken away. Transience is the name of the game in life. This is not necessarily negative or dismal. It is truth. And, thank God, God is with us in the midst of this truth, life's brevity and its sweet, sweet strangeness.

There is no sense in lamenting too much the wounding nature of the world. Sheer existence, the fact that there is *something* rather than *nothing*, is a gift, a gift whom even Job (of all people!) concludes we ought to give thanks and praise for when things are given *and even when things are taken away*. This is a challenging word for us, but it is a good word nonetheless. Richard Rohr puts the point this way: "Necessary suffering goes on every day, seemingly without question. . . . I just read that only one saguaro cactus seed out of a quarter of a million seeds ever makes it even to early maturity, and even fewer after that. Most of nature seems to totally accept major loss, gross inefficiency, mass extinctions, and short life spans as the price of life at all. Feeling that sadness, and even its full absurdity, ironically pulls us into the general dance, the unified field, an ironic and deep gratitude for what *is* given—with no necessity and so gratuitously. All beauty is gratuitous. So whom can we blame when it seems to be taken away? Grace seems to be at the foundation of everything."[6]

4. Ibid.
5. Gibran, *The Prophet*, 17.
6. Rohr, *Falling Upward*, 77–78.

When people or things leave us and we are wounded there is not only pain. There is a way in which "leaving creates space for God's spirit . . ."[7] Henri Nouwen observes. There is a way in which, by absence, God can become present, in a new way.[8] During my week of rest and healing I discovered just how true this is. It was only in the midst of a week of sudden emptiness that I was able to see and then attend to some inner wounds. When we bring loving attentiveness to our inner wounds, as naturally as we do to our outer physical wounds, there is a gentle healing that begins.

I heard a wonderful story recently about Frank Lloyd Wright, the famous American architect. He was walking along as a child one day with his uncle through a snow-covered field. They were on their way to a friend's house. But along the way Frank wandered off the path, taking in the sights. He stopped at a barn to see the animals. He then wandered over to a pond and lingered there for a while. Next he saw a fort off in the distance and took a moment to investigate. Finally he caught up with his uncle who said to him, "Frank, I have an important lesson for you to learn. Look back at our footsteps in the snow. Mine came *straight here*. I never ventured off the path, and I arrived here much quicker than you. But look at yours! You zigzagged all over the place and wasted so much time stopping at different points along the way." Frank Lloyd Wright would later say it was one of the best lessons he ever learned, though not in the way his uncle had intended. Frank took the lesson in just the opposite way. His take was, "I still arrived at the same destination. But, better yet, I got to enjoy all the wonderful sights by wandering along the way."

Wandering is sometimes just what we need for our wounds. In the nothingness and aimlessness of wandering, we can find time just to breathe, to be, to reflect, and to enjoy the moment, instead of relentlessly *working, working, working* towards some goal, while missing the beautiful things along the way. Wandering inwardly is a gentle, non-analytical, non-intrusive way to approach our wounds. The neglected areas of our inward journey crying out for

7. Nouwen, *The Living Reminder*, 44.

8. Ibid., 44.

healing need a friendly approach. Allowing the mind to wander over them, without judgment, without guilt for mistakes we have made, opens up space for our wounds to come out of the dark into the healing light of day. Simply and compassionately acknowledging our woundedness, alongside the unwounded areas of our lives, brings healing by allowing us to begin seeing a way to accept and integrate all of our experiences. It is the refusal to accept and integrate our wounded areas that so often prevents healing.

But we can go a step further. Beyond integration, we need to see that the dark and light, the sorrowful and joyful moments of our lives, are inextricably connected.

The Taoist master Chuang Tzu illustrates this truth in a story about an old man whose wife dies after many years happily together. Just like that, she is suddenly taken away. The children who live in the village across the mountains become concerned when they learn of their mother's passing but haven't heard a single word from their father. One morning, they decide to trek the half-day journey across the mountains to the small hut where their father lives. When they arrive, they knock three times on his door. But there is no reply. They knock again. Still, nothing, though from inside they can faintly hear some kind of racket. They decide to open the door and enter on their own. When they do, what they see shocks and bewilders them. There is their father seated on the floor in the kitchen, banging on pots and pans, singing and playing as loudly as he possibly can as if celebrating! They are confused, but their confusion quickly morphs into anger. "What on earth are you doing?" one of them hollers. "*Our* mother, *your* wife of many years, has left us! And here you are celebrating! What's the matter with you?" The old man stops what he is doing and slowly looks up at his children. Then he speaks, cautiously, "At first, I did mourn. I mourned deeply. It was a hard time. But, then, I realized that to continue only in grief would be to proclaim myself ignorant of the great way of things, that we all enter this world with nothing and we leave with nothing, that we come from, and return to, the very same Source, that all of our joys are tied to our sorrows, and our sorrows to our joys. This is the way of things."

Chuang Tzu reminds me of Joseph who, at the end of the Old Testament book of Genesis, shares a similarly great insight with us. Joseph's brothers had sold him into slavery over their resentment for who he was and the cherished place he held in their father's heart. This disastrous turn of events was surely not the future Joseph had expected. He is wounded. Yet, not unlike Frank Lloyd Wright, Joseph learns an unintended lesson. Joseph, having worked through tragedy and eventually come into a season of great abundance where he is able to feed those who would have otherwise starved to death during a famine, says to his brothers, "You intended to harm me, *but God intended it for good* to accomplish what is now being done, the saving of many lives."[9] Something intended for harm God enigmatically uses for good.

It's important to notice that the story does *not* say evil does not happen. Evil most certainly does, as Joseph experienced. Experience wounds us. Our wounds are real. Joseph's insight, however, emphasizes how salvation ("the saving of many lives") so often happens at the *nexus* of the good and the bad, not only one or the other. Joy and sorrow in this way are strangely, and intimately, connected. Kahlil Gibran pens words that Joseph himself could have written and which deserve to be read slowly: "Your joy is your sorrow unmasked. And the selfsame well from which your laughter rises was oftentimes filled with your tears. And how else can it be? The deeper that sorrow carves into your being the more joy you can contain. Is not the cup that holds your wine the very cup that was burned in the potter's oven? And is not the lute that soothes your spirit, the very wood that was hollowed with knives? When you are joyous, look deep into your heart and you shall find it is only that which has given you sorrow that is giving you joy. When you are sorrowful look again in your heart, and you shall see that in truth you are weeping for that which has been your delight."[10]

9. Gen 50:20, italics added.

10. Gibran, *The Prophet*, 29.

16

ON BEING

Suffering comes in so many different forms. Some suffer from violence and war even at this very moment as you read these words. Others right now are suffering from the natural process of aging, the aches and pains that go in tandem with the fading of this life. If I put on my prophetic hat for a moment I would surmise that you, too, in some form are suffering right now as well. How could I possibly know that? I know that because there is no life without suffering. Suffering is constitutive of life. None of us escapes its clutches.

One form of suffering that I have been aquatinted with is acedia. Acedia admittedly is hard to describe. It is something *like* depression, a pressing down of the spirit, though it is not depression. The mystics of Christianity have called it a "listlessness," a melancholy darkness of the soul that can submerge us for a season, a feeling that everything may very well be meaningless, even if one in faith knows better, even if one knows God. Acedia is a weariness with life.[1] And for no apparent reason. That's an important feature of acedia. Your life can be graced with amazing things, dotted with blessings galore, and yet you still feel this nagging, gnawing sense

1. Bunge, *Despondency*, 45–46.

that something vital is absent. Acedia can sneak up on us even and especially when most all else in life seems good, pleasant, and bright. This is why it was given the ancient designation "the noonday demon."[2]

Acedia, though a thoroughly unfamiliar term to most modern ears, may very well be the unnamed evil of our time. From what I have observed as a pastor, teacher, sometimes counselor, confidant, and general observer of this funny bunch we call the human race, acedia is affecting more and more today than you might guess. There is a general malaise covering over many peoples' lives. Slow and syrupy like, it pours over us with discontent, and though we don't often know why, its stickiness makes it downright difficult to clean off. Is it our disenchantment with the failed promise of happiness implicit in our consumeristic tendencies that feeds the darkness of acedia, always seeking more, yet feeling more and more like we have less, feeling empty? Could it be a by-product of narcissism? Or maybe it's the inevitable consequence of living in an increasingly smaller global village, conscious of the radically different meaning systems available to us, and therefore the possibility that none of them really knows much of anything absolutely when all is said and done? Whatever the reasons, it seems more than a few of us today are acquainted with this form of emptiness.

When we find ourselves to be in an acediac place, rather than turning away from it, sometimes the very best thing to do is to go with it, to allow oneself to simply "be" in the emptiness that is whelming or even overwhelming us. This has been a hard lesson for me to learn. But emptiness can be a teacher. Rather than fighting fruitlessly against it, we can allow the emptying to be something more than only a form of suffering. When we allow ourselves to be in the emptiness and to let go even temporarily of so many of the things we think are important, yet which all fade into Oblivion, it is then that we can see what if anything remains. What does remain is priceless.

It was a normal day for me one Tuesday not too many years ago, a normal day at least to the casual eye and from an outsider's

2. Nault, *The Noonday Devil*, 11, 20.

point of view, even a good day. Work had been productive. I was recently married. Erin and I were enjoying living on our own in our very first one-bedroom apartment, a quaint dwelling of 590 square feet that I still remember fondly. As the day progressed, however, and for no particular reason, I felt increasingly swept away with despondent thoughts and a deepening sense of emptiness. I am psychologically healthy so I knew I wasn't losing my mind. Though it might have been tempting or maybe even appropriate for another individual to write this off as a neurological imbalance I simply couldn't do that. This was also not the first time I had been acquainted with the hollowing (and hallowing?) of acedia, though I did not know it by that name at the time. On this particular Tuesday I decided to do something different as the black hole sought to pull me in: I went with it. I chose to allow the emptying to happen instead of fighting it. It scared the hell out of me. And it hurt.

By the day's end, while Erin was away that night at a small group with some of her girlfriends, I was alone and in an utterly abandoned place. If faith is not faith without entertaining the possibility of despairing over life and it's raw mystery, then this was a day in which I had allowed myself perhaps for the first time to fully feel such despair. Then something remarkable happened. Love. It was utterly unexpected. Something remained in me after I had felt emptied of so much. It was, to force it into a single word, love. My love for God, and my love for Erin, remained. That love remaining so pure and simple was like a light in the darkness, a light that not only has continued to illuminate my path in the days following that Tuesday, but a light that has taught me the blessing of emptiness. As Kathleen Norris notes in her own research and experience of acedia, "Monastic wisdom insists that when we are most tempted to feel bored, apathetic, and despondent over the meaninglessness of life we are on the verge of discovering our true self in relation to God. It is worth not giving up, because when we are willing to do nothing but 'be,' we meet the God who is the very ground of being, the great 'I Am' whom Moses encountered at the burning bush."[3]

3. Norris, *Acedia & me*, 40–41.

Embracing our being, even in our sufferings, is essential to our flourishing. Yet we have largely forgotten how to be. Indeed, if one were to bring up the topic of "being" with your average person these days many would respond with a raised eyebrow and puzzlement. "Being?" we might ask. "What does *that* mean?" *Doing* is something we can talk about all day long precisely because we do so much. But we are not the sum total of what we do though our actions define us to an extent. Beyond our activities we are human *beings*. *You* have a unique nature, just as *I* have a unique nature. There is something in you that makes you *you* in your being and there is no other like you. To be in touch with your own being is a bountiful experience—even one that brings us to the brink of knowing the divine. As John Calvin put it so eloquently, to know thyself is also to know the One who made thyself.[4]

I tell my family this regularly. Isabella is bright, precocious, marked by beauty inside and out. She is deeply caring. She has an enthusiasm for life that is remarkable. I learn from her whenever I catch glimpses of her passion bubbling to the surface, which is often. My son Joshua is wild at heart, a true boy, uncontainable in his zest for laughing and silliness to no end for no reason at all (which is always the very best reason to cut loose and to *be* silly). He has an uncanny eye for patterns, organization, and fitting things together like I've never seen in someone so young, and I affirm this verbally to him often so that, hopefully, he will never forget that his being is precious, a hallmark of the glory of God right here on earth. My lovely wife, Erin, whom I call Air, is, interestingly, very much like the air element, a blessing to me and to many others: lovely, soothing, mysterious, magnanimous.

Being acquainted with your being is no small thing, even if a rather unfamiliar thing for too many of us. Sometimes we avoid being because of the darkness we're afraid we might encounter within. Other times we're simply impatient and fancy ourselves too busy with more "important" things. The skeptic inside us wants to know *why* doing something as utterly basic as being for any length of time is something so important and good for us to

4. Calvin, *Institutes of the Christian Religion*, 35.

enjoy. Honestly, I cannot say exactly why being is so good and so important for us to be acquainted with, nor is it a point I wish to find too many reasons to advance. The importance of being is more an intuition that arises. I suspect if you give it a chance, it is one that might awaken something new and powerful within you as well.

"How can I become better acquainted with being?" you might ask. Well, doing nothing is one good way, and a joyfully iconoclastic one at that. Though if we are unpracticed in doing nothing the "work self" and the "productive self" and the other such "selves" that occupy the space within us may very well protest against the idea of doing nothing. To paraphrase the humorist Ian Frazier, "The only way we could justify sitting motionless in an A-frame cabin in the woods was if we had just survived a really messy divorce." That is to say, modern people have real trouble with the idea of doing nothing and especially with the idea of doing nothing being a virtuous activity, or even neutrally okay, so much so that we feel like we need an excuse to do nothing, such as having just gone through a messy divorce. If we have a reason, if we have an excuse, then and only then does doing nothing become permissible. The potential guilt over doing nothing would then be small, and any potential criticism from others marginalized.

Author and psychotherapist David Kundtz, in commenting on Frazier's words here writes, "But then [Frazier] wisely throws out that kind of thinking and gives himself permission—no justification necessary—for doing nothing. Unnecessary self-restrictions and false guilt burden many of us and keep us from the peaceful times we yearn for. Quiet time to be alone is not an optional nicety; nor is it just for the retired, the lazy, or those naturally inclined. It is for all of us. It is valuable time well spent. And above all, it needs no justification other than its own noble purpose: to become more fully awake and to remember what you most need to remember about yourself and your life."[5]

Can you remember the last time you did nothing, even for a little while? The idea of doing nothing as a virtue is not new.

5. Kundtz, *Moments In Between*, 14.

In Taoist thought the idea is called *wu wei* or *wei wu wei*, literally, "doing not-doing." *Wu wei* does not mean passively sitting by while injustices mount and the good work to be done in the world passes us by. *Wu wei* does mean doing *from* a place of being, in touch with your unique being. To do, do, do yet be unfamiliar with the self that is doing is to commit violence against yourself. But to do from a place of being, in touch with your being, is to live compassionately toward others and yourself. It is surprising, even at times amazing, to catch glimpses of the goodness that can arise out of doing nothing.

This was true of Elias Howe, who lived in the 1800s and is credited with inventing the sewing machine. One day, as Howe was working on his sewing machine project, so the story goes, he became especially frustrated. Things weren't working. He had been working with a regular sewing needle and had attempted several different ways to mechanize it, with no success. So, he eventually decided to stop and take a break from his efforts. He sat down at the window of his workshop, gazing aimlessly for a while at the expanse of the horizon. He later told his wife about what happened next: "As I wandered in my mind, a remarkable scene came to me. I was in a deep jungle and I was in a big, black pot with a roaring fire under it. I was being cooked alive! A warrior came at me with spear raised and ready to thrust. But what I noticed at that moment was something very curious about the spear: It had a hole in its tip."[6] The crucial discovery that led to the invention of the sewing machine is that the hole for the thread goes in the tip of the needle, not at its other end as in a regular needle. It is a deep and delightful irony that so often creativity and productivity need the dark soil of nothingness: a wandering mind, not doing, simply being.

6. Ibid., 21.

17

VANISHING

I was teaching philosophy and religion at Sacred Heart University in Connecticut when I received a student's paper during midterms that felt a little too polished, even familiar. Sure enough, after doing a bit of digging I discovered the student had plagiarized almost the entire essay. When I approached him about it after class one day his response could not have been more apathetic. I said, "I'll have to give you a failing grade you know. I really don't want to but you've tied my hands." Before quickly walking away he replied, nonchalantly, "Oh well."

We sometimes hear our elders lament over the flippant ways of young people today, the evaporation of morals, and general decay of society. They reminisce about the good old days when things were built to last, you could leave your front door unlocked, and kids knew how to address their seniors. Though it is a bit naïve to overestimate the actual goodness of the "good old days" (there have always been great ills in every age) there is a grain of truth to the sentiment. Things *are* vanishing.

There are 7,120 identified languages in the world, an incomplete list because of ongoing discoveries, and half of them are endangered. *Half* will vanish in this century alone. The Koro language of India, for instance, has less than 1,000 speakers left. The Native American language of Siletz is worse off yet with just one speaker remaining. Linguistic extinction is the order of the day.

Likewise, farming is vanishing as a way of life in America. A hundred years ago one in three Americans were farmers. Today it's one in one hundred.

Technologically, in the world of the internet, things are constantly moving into nothingness. Vint Cerf, one of the fathers of the internet and currently vice president at Google, wonders if people in the twenty-second century will have access to the history of our blogs, websites, emails, tweets, and so on here at the dawn of the twenty-first century, or more likely, will all of it have evaporated into a foggy, digital darkness? To those who might wonder "so what?" if it does evaporate, it is important to realize how unprecedented this is. People have long recorded their histories, chiseled into stone, painted on papyrus, or written down on paper. But now, suddenly, in this new digital frontier, our knowledge is vanishing just as quickly as it appears. What does this do over long periods of time to our collective sense of history as a species? An important question as the pace of change seems to wind irrevocably faster and faster.

Church life is also experiencing a vanishing, not only in membership (the United Church of Christ, for example, has lost approximately 1,000,000 members since the 1960s), but also in terms of biblical literacy. Not so long ago a pastor could have said to his or her congregation on a Sunday, "You know the story about Daniel in the _____" and people would have filled in the blank with "Lion's Den!" like a chorus. Now, it's not at all uncommon for the blank space to remain just that.

Churches in Britain, Scotland, and elsewhere are being transformed into laundromats, condos, and even bars. Today less than one tenth of British adults are attending church of any kind. So many of the arrows on charts are pointing downward regarding the religious: decreases in the frequency of prayer, belief in God,

Sunday attendance, church membership, the list goes on and on. The rise of irreligion is historically unprecedented. More and more Americans identify themselves as "nones," with 89 percent of them saying they are *not* looking for a religion to join.

Fewer than 5 percent of Americans back in the 1950s were nonreligious. By the 1990s that figure had changed to 8 percent. Then it jumped to 14 percent in 2001, 16 percent in 2010, 19 percent in 2013, and as of the most recent national surveys, it is up to 30 percent today.[1]

Some of the reasons for this trend are what we might guess: reaction to the Catholic priests sex abuse scandal, the backlash of the success of the religious right that has by-and-large religiously disenchanted the next generation. But some of the causes were unanticipated, such as the increased number of women joining the paid labor force contributing to the rise of secularism. The jury is still out on the *interpretation* of the research clearly indicating such trends. Perhaps families are too tired to attend worship more often on the weekends now with both parents working, or is it more a decrease in the need for psychological and social support that churches are often seen as providing because women are getting that support elsewhere now, or some combination of factors? Whatever the reasons, it seems there is a kernel of truth to the notion that it's mostly our moms who are (or were) getting us out of bed on Sundays.

At the end of a lecture I was attending where sociologist Phil Zuckerman detailed some of this data, the woman seated next to me murmured, "How discouraging." "No," I quickly replied, containing my zeal as much as possible. "It is, what is." I wasn't discouraged or worried, even as a pastor, about this current state of affairs. Why should I be? God watches over us still. Always has. Always will. As I walked home I was reminded of an important point of convergence between Taoist and biblical wisdom. Ecclesiastes writes in about the third century BCE, "For everything there is a season, and a time for every matter under heaven . . . a time to break down, and a time to build up . . . a time to seek, and a time

1. Zuckerman, *Living the Secular Life*, 5.

to lose; a time to keep, and a time to cast away."[2] It is interesting that more than four thousand miles away, at about the same time Ecclesiastes wrote this, Chuang Tzu in China unknowingly wrote something quite similar: "There is a time for putting together and another time for taking apart. He who understands this course of events takes each new state in its proper time with neither sorrow nor joy. . . . Where is there a reason to be discouraged?"[3]

There is no reason to be discouraged in the midst of life's metamorphoses. All things move toward absence. They vanish, each and every one of them, eventually. Change is paradoxically the great constant. Yet it's so important to remember that with change comes not only vanishing but also the *emerging* of new things. The beauty of loss is the room it makes for something new. Fall to winter, and winter to spring. Life to death, and death to resurrection. Twilight to night, and night to a new dawn. Vanishing is the sister of emergence.[4] This is the way of things and there is no sense in lamenting or celebrating it. Rather, we must embrace it. Accept it. Even more than that, be in tune with it. Give thanks for the things you have and the people you love! They are not here forever. Be patient with the trials to come. They are not here forever either. Know that the fading of the "good" and "bad" is making room for the emergence of something new for you. The gift of absence always contains a secret blessing.

---

2. Eccl 3:1, 3, 6.

3. Merton, *The Way of Chuang Tzu*, 63–64.

4. O'Donohue, *Eternal Echoes*, 240.

18

THE PASTOR WHO CHASED ME
DOWN THE STREET

One of the criticisms you're likely to hear these days in religious circles, sometimes leveled by religious fundamentalists against more open-minded believers, is a criticism about so-called pick-and-choose religion. "You can't simply pick and choose what you want to believe from the Bible," the argument goes, "because if everyone did that then all you would have is a religion made in your own image. You've got to accept the whole thing as it is! It's all or nothing." As a pastor myself you might expect me to agree with this and to preach something similar. But I do not agree with this line of thought at all. Nor will I attempt to "preach" much of anything to you. True wisdom any of us might have to share with one another will always be clear, even intriguing, never something that needs to be walloped over the head.

It's true there is some merit to this criticism about pick-and-choose religion. If every Christian simply believed whatever they wanted to believe from the faith, trimmed of the excesses of those commands we deem unfashionable, undesirable, or too challenging, we'd be left with fake religion indeed, one geared at nothing more than mere self-satisfaction. The value of this line of thought ends here.

The truth is that everyone to some extent picks and chooses what they believe. Of course they do. How could we not as creatures imbued with volition making literally thousands of choices every single day? We are selective creatures by nature. We may inherit this and that. Still we constantly make choices, conscious and tacit, overt and subtle, that shape what we experience, what we believe, and the course of our lives. The notion of someone (anyone) who doesn't pick and choose what they believe to some extent is absurd. Can you honestly imagine what a real flesh-and-blood human being would even look like who attempted to believe the *whole* Bible hook, line, and sinker? Believe it or not, at least one man actually did attempt this. The results did not turn out so well.

The always entertaining A. J. Jacobs chronicles his 365 days of attempting to live by the rules of the Bible, unbiased, without picking and choosing, in *The Year of Living Biblically: One Man's Humble Quest to Follow the Bible as Literally as Possible.* Jacobs grew a long beard according to one biblical rule. He threw out all of his clothing made with mixed fibers according to another teaching. His wife even gave birth to twins during the experiment, according to the Genesis command to be fruitful and multiply. Fortunately, it seems, they were planning on having kids anyway.

These are just a few examples on the tip of an iceberg of absurdity in Jacobs' attempt to *not* pick and choose when it comes to the Bible. What Jacobs' yearlong experiment reveals is what happens when you take this notion that "real believers" don't pick and choose to its logical conclusion, namely, something like foolishness, plain and simple. All of the Bible's commands do not fit neatly together, in part due to the nature of multiple authors composing various books in the Bible at various times throughout history, and so what you end up with if you *assume* uniformity and attempt to follow *every* injunction without choosing or prioritizing is an unnecessary absurdity. Those religious fundamentalists who say they read the Bible literally (as high as 45 percent of Americans in some polls) are, actually, picking and choosing as much as anyone else when it comes to the Bible and what they profess to believe—even if they are reticent to admit as much.

If this is the case, as it clearly seems to be, then why do so many still adamantly insist on this "take it or leave it" approach when it comes to the Bible? The reason, by and large, is fear. If we admit there is a selection process going on in what we believe, the fear is that faith appears ambiguous, or worse, arbitrary, and that is a slippery slope. If we don't have something absolutely certain and clear-cut to stand on for moral authority and daily living the anxiety is that everything will go to hell in a hand basket.

But that's simply not true. And even if it were true, we still can't deny the element of choice so obviously operative in the shaping of our beliefs. Besides, *absolute* certainty is nothing more than an illusion in this life anyway. If you can argue one thing, there is always someone else who can argue the exact opposite, and with just as much reason and intensity. Absolute certainty is a myth. No sense in trying to base your life on something that just isn't there. You have to work from what is there. And what *is* there as we are realizing more and more in our day and age is the *absence* of clear-cut rules.

For so many people today, if you tell them that you do such and such because "the Bible tells you to" they will look at you like you're crazy. That doesn't mean they're right (or wrong). It does mean, however, that gone are the days when we could teach our children to do this or that because it's written down somewhere to do this or that and expect that they will do this or that unquestioningly. Human beings are wonderfully reflective creatures.

Likewise, gone are the days when many go to church on Sundays only because it's presumed to be the thing to do: go, listen, and obey. The cultural tempo has changed—radically. Whether for good or ill, ultimately, that is for history to say. But whether or not we believe that the commands of the Bible are ironclad and beyond reflection, *teaching* them as such is no longer tenable. That kind of teaching will fall on too many deaf ears. And those who do uncritically listen and obey, as we see with someone like A. J. Jacobs, are simply being duped with nonsense. The staunch approach to religion that tends to see life in black and white simply doesn't ring true to life's many shades of grey. Yet it seems there are always those who will clench to a narrow field of vision.

I was on foot to a clergy luncheon one afternoon at a place I hadn't been to before. I accidentally went to the wrong building at first. When I entered, there happened to be another pastor standing there as I pulled out my map to get my bearings. He was much older than me. If I had to guess, he was at least in his eighties, if not older, with a rather stoic look on his face and a dry English accent. "Here now," he said to me, "let me help you with that." I was about to be late to my gathering, with only a minute or so to spare, and was pretty sure now about where I needed to go. But, not wanting to be rude, I replied hesitantly, "Okay. But I think I know where I'm going now and I really can't be late." He seemed to ignore my comment as he slowly began to peer over the map. And then to look over the map some more. And then to look it over yet some more. After seriously, literally, at least two full minutes if not more I turned to him and said as kindly as I could, "It's okay. I've really got to go. I'll find it easily enough. No worries. Thank you."

But as I began to head for the door he grabbed my arm— which startled me. I'm not accustomed to strangers grabbing my arm and rather firmly at that. "Now hold on there," he said. "I can help you." I'm sure he could have helped me, if I had the luxury of time. Yet not wanting to come across as some rude whippersnapper rushing about like so many young people do these days, I decided against my better judgment to give him another half minute before I was finally forced to say, with a smile, "I'm sorry, but I really must be going now."

I had done my due diligence with regards to etiquette, I thought, as I exited through the front door. But the man was unrelenting and wouldn't let me go! "Now hold on," the pastor hollered as I went down the front steps toward the sidewalk. "Hold on *one minute!*" I offered another friendly smile as I continued walking, as if to say, it's okay, but I really need to go. To my astonishment, he continued after me! He followed me out of the house, down the front stairs, and onto the sidewalk! Another twenty paces, I glanced back, and he was *still* hollering and chasing after me. This was ludicrous! Fortunately, I was faster, eventually lost him, and made it to my luncheon just before the blessing for the meal.

What on earth was this all about? I'm sorry that I can't tell you because I honestly don't know. But I do know this: *too many Christians are accustomed to using just this kind of approach to communicate what they think they know about the gospel*, and in today's world so very many respond exactly like I did. They run the other way.

How we *approach* others in life is so important. This is very true of how we share our faith with one another as well. If *not* sharing our faith much at all, so often out of fear of judgment or ridicule, is one extreme, then the other extreme is sharing our faith dogmatically, inflexibly, insistently, with the presumption of having all the right answers but none of the right questions. The pendulum can easily swing far in either direction, if we're not careful, and we do need to be care-full (full of care) in how we share the gift of our faith. The good news of God's love is too precious *not* to share but likewise too lovely to misshape and share intrusively. The gospel is inherently intriguing. It doesn't need the presumption and loose logic of legalism. The gift of faith, and your particular understanding and rendering of faith, is just that, a gift. It is a gift characterized by convictions and questions, knowing and not knowing, about some of the most vital matters of existence. Your faith is a beautiful gift for sharing even in its incompleteness, tentativeness, confidence, and uncertainty.

When my wife Erin and I share our faith with our children we are quite honest with them about what we are passionate about, what we are committed to, what we believe (and why), but just as forthcoming with them about our questions and what we don't understand. It's important for them to know that we don't have it all figured out. It's important for them to know there's Mystery in the universe! And that this is a wonderful thing. When we pray, there's often smiling and laughter in addition to solemn moments.

When we discuss Jesus and God and the Bible, there are as many questions posed as answers. Above all, what we try to teach our children, more than a list of rules, is the gospel's essence, both in word and deed. Christianity at its best has always been about identifying and living this essence, going back to Jesus who, masterfully, paired faith down to its essence when he said unequivocally that the entire law and the prophets (all of it) are summed up in this: love.[1] *Love.* Jesus wanted his followers to move beyond the mere letter of God's law to the spirit of the law, its essence.[2] In other words, don't allow yourself to get lost in the minutia of religion and for heaven's sake don't forget that its essence is to be communicated, lovingly, every single day. Both the *substance* of our message and the *approach* should be the same. Love. Love God. Love others. It is our *raison d'être.*

---

1. Matt 22:37–40; Gal 5:14.
2. Mark 3:1–6; Rom 2:28–29; 2 Cor 3:6.

19

EREMITIC

There's a story about a rabbi who lived as a hermit in a small cottage in the woods. The rabbi had no chairs or stools to sit on, no furniture whatsoever, except for a solitary desk that also served as his bed at night. One day, to his surprise, the rabbi had a visitor. Upon entering the rabbi's humble abode and looking around at the simplicity of the surroundings, not knowing where to sit or what to do with himself, the visitor remarked pensively, "Where is your furniture?" The rabbi replied, "Where is yours?" "I don't have any," said the perplexed visitor. "I'm only passing through." "So am I," said the rabbi. "So am I."

One of the gifts of allowing a bit more absence into our lives is a deepening knowledge of the transience of life. Transience makes a ghost of every experience. The future of every moment is its disappearance.[1] Like the visitor, and the rabbi, we are all just "passing through." It is important to sit with this reality. Life and everything with it is fleeting. This is no morbid thought. It is truth, the truth about the fragility of your life and mine here on this earth.

1. O'Donohue, *Four Elements*, 152.

Practicing absence—enjoying the presence but also the absence of material possessions, the presence but also the absence of community and communication—can bring this truth more clearly into focus for us. Going for a walk now and then alone. Eating our lunch occasionally in solitude. Taking a weekend to go off, rest, and pray. Such absence opens the eyes. It helps us to live our lives fully and more fully awake.

Hermits within our spiritual traditions knew this quite well. It's why people like Saint Jerome would dare such audacious acts as committing himself to years in solitude. Though that practice seems extreme to most of us today, we find that in days past the way of aloneness was favorably recounted and gently recommended. The Hebrew culture relayed to us through the Hebrew Scriptures, for instance, reflects to us not only the gift of togetherness but also the counter-cultural gift of the eremitic. One reads the Old Testament and cannot help but come away with a profound sense of the richness of community in the history of the Hebrew people. Yet, likewise, simultaneously, there is an undeniable emphasis on the beauty and blessedness of solitude. Genesis reminds us that it was not good for man to be alone[2] but Exodus quickly follows, highlighting one, Moses, who spent days upon days on the mountaintop alone with his God.[3] Ecclesiastes reminds us, "If two lie down together, they will keep warm. But how can one keep warm alone? Though one may be overpowered, two can defend themselves. A cord of three strands is not quickly broken."[4] Yet complementing this perspective we cannot miss the brilliant examples of Jacob[5] and Elijah[6] with whom God spoke only once they had space to be alone.

Scripture highlights both. If we find ourselves emphasizing one over the other, this is only a revelation of our own bias, preference, and inclination.

2. Gen 2:18.
3. Exod 34:28.
4. Eccl 4:11–12.
5. Gen 32:24–32.
6. 1 Kgs 19:9–18.

There is a place both for being with and apart from others. To Dietrich Bonhoeffer's affirmation of the joys of being with other people in his *Life Together* there is the fair counterpoint that surely any of us can relate to at least on some days, stated pithily in Jean-Paul Sartre's *No Exit*: "Hell is just—other people."[7]

As I write this I am on study leave, away from my family, friends, and church community. I am close to ecstatic! Well, not really, not entirely. I say this tongue in cheek. My ecstasy is not only because I am away for a time from the pressures of work for a respite. I love my church family. Nor is my gladness rooted especially in being away from my children, whom I love dearly, yet whose periodic teasing, whining, and fighting can wear on any parent after a while. I have always been more of a recluse. Though not radically so, I have a strong strain of introversion that contributes to the strength of who I am. I need ample time for quiet and solitude. My Meyers-Briggs assessment plots me as "The Protector" INFJ personality type, which means I enjoy shepherding others, among other things, and thus I am well suited to my profession as a teacher and pastor. But the wellspring of my vitality is rooted in reclusion. I need nothingness. Time alone suits me well.

Yet it's not only the introverts among us who are served well by intervals of absence from interaction—cyber-like, interpersonally, and so on. I heard a wonderful lecture given by Susan Cain (who is herself an introvert) on the power of introversion for any of us. This is a challenging word, for we live in a culture biased toward thinking of extroversion positively, and introversion negatively. This is an unfortunate misunderstanding. There are tremendous gifts to both ways of being and the balanced mind understands that each has something to learn from the other.

Though we are each alone in this world, it takes great courage to meet with the full force of your aloneness. Until you learn to inhabit your aloneness, the lonely distractions of society will continually seduce you into false senses of belonging that only leave you empty and weary. Facing your aloneness changes you. Gradually, something begins to happen inside you. The sense of bleakness

7. Sartre, *No Exit*, 52.

changes into a sense of true belonging wherein you eventually and increasingly come into rhythm with the uniqueness of your own life. This is slow work.[8] Indeed, in a sense, it is an ongoing unraveling of homecoming that spans your entire life.

Rattling off statistics on the many benefits of being away from others, and disconnecting from others technologically often enough as well, is less fruitful than *experiencing* absence a bit more yourself.[9] There's nothing quite like tasting and seeing for yourself such transcendent goodness.[10] If you are an extrovert, at first this will probably be more of an exercise and stretch for you. Be patient with yourself. If you easily gravitate inward, then this may come more naturally. Either way—whether with ease or effort, extrovert or introvert—we can each expect a gentle unfolding of goodness within as we allow ourselves fellowship with absence. There is a blessing in absence, one that restores the soul, which the busy avoid but the wise seek. It takes time before we begin to notice this goodness. But if we dare to disconnect, even a bit more in this quintessentially connected age, we can come closer to knowing ourselves, God, and yes, even joy. Scripture encourages us: "The Lord is good to those whose hope is in him, to the one who seeks him; it is good to wait quietly for the salvation of the Lord. Let him sit alone in silence."[11]

---

8. O'Donohue, *Eternal Echoes*, 93.

9. Dr. Ryan Martin of the University of Wisconsin has found that over-communicating through text messages, for example, can decrease a person's sense of identity.

10. Ps 34:8.

11. Lam 3:25–26, 28a.

20

READING SCRIPTURE WITH THE SPACES IN
BETWEEN

My wife leads a morning devotional time with our children during the school week. I sometimes join in before I head out the door to work. It's great stuff. Erin spends just five minutes sharing a story from the Bible and then opening up a brief conversation about it. I admire the way she engages them. Both Bella and Josh are genuinely excited about the stories and what the Bible has to say—which is no small thing, even for two pastor's kids, given the numerous other pulls on their attention these days. Part of the reason they look forward to this time is because they know from both Erin and I (and not just in words) that there is something special about this book. They're intrigued by what that might be, and what the lessons and stories of this great book have to show them about this mysterious one we call "God." But beyond this conviction in the specialness, call it the *sacredness* of the text—a conviction that Christians of all ages have shared because of the experience of God continually revealing himself to his people through *this* text more so than through any other text— their enthusiasm for engaging the Word of God each morning, I've noticed, also has as much to do with *how* they come at the text and what they notice is present (or not present) in the text.

Sometimes, sure, there is a moral teaching in the story that catches their attention plain and simple. But just as often what captivates them is what the stories leave out. What is *not* in the text, in tandem with what *is* in the text, has a tendency to inspire wondering and multiple understandings of the meanings (plural, not singular) in the text.

For everything that is mentioned in the text there is something that is not mentioned, something that is absent, at times unintentional and at other times it seems intentional in order to make room for that which *is* present in the biblical text. My children have learned to have eyes for this, as have I, and truly it's not only instructive but also great fun exploring these absences in the text, wandering through them, and wondering in them. These absences are like wonderful black holes that pull us in with their curiosity and gravity such that we engage the Bible more deeply.

In the children's Bible that Erin reads from, for example, she and the kids recently came to the story of Abraham's call to sacrifice his son Isaac in Genesis 22.[1] The story in part is about how God provides (Jehovah Jireh).[2] God provides a ram, in the thicket, just in the nick of time for Abraham to sacrifice *instead* of his son (thank God). And then, for his faith and willingness to do even the unthinkable for God, the story says that Abraham received a "great reward."[3] It's interesting that the story does *not* provide any additional details about this "great reward," what is often translated in our adult versions of the Bible as Abraham's "blessing." But as soon as we finished reading the story my son had to know, exclaiming, "What was the reward?"

---

1. How fascinating how many versions of the Bible supposedly adapted for children nevertheless make the choice to retain some of the most graphic, potentially nightmarish stories! Though I suppose one cannot dilute the Bible too much even for children, lest we not have much of anything left to read. The Bible is a radical book. It is the furthest thing from the occasional complaints leveled against it of being "bland" or "boring." Not true!

2. Gen 22:14.

3. Gen 22:15–18.

It's a great question for any of us regarding this important story. Is the "reward" the promise of descendants more numerous than the stars of the sky and the sand on the seashore? Indeed, this is how many of us read the story. Yet it is not entirely clear that this is the intended meaning of the text or the only way we can or should read it. The text juxtaposes Abraham receiving a reward or blessing next to God's promise to grant descendants more numerous than one can count. But that does not mean that the former equates with the latter. Is the "reward" perhaps more simply the gift of Isaac's longevity? The story entails a bit of ambiguity, as highlighted by the children's version of the Bible my wife was reading from, and we as the readers are invited by this lack of clarity into a place of wondering. What *does* a reward, from God, look like? What does a reward mean in the context of God's audacious request for Abraham to sacrifice his own son? Whether it's my son playfully wondering about this mysterious reward (perhaps because he has a "reward jar" that gets filled with marbles each day leading to a small reward for his good behavior), or whether it's you and me wondering about the depths of meaning here in a text that Soren Kierkegaard regarded with "fear and trembling," either way, the *wondering* is a marvelous thing. Such questioning and conversation with the text is a way of keeping the text alive to us and us alive to the text, inviting the Holy Spirit to speak dynamically to us through the text.

In Medieval Europe, some cathedrals had what are known as "Holy Spirit holes." These actual holes, drilled into the ceilings of the cathedrals, served as a symbolic reminder that the Holy Spirit can *never* be contained, not even by the church. The nature of God is uncircumscribable. During Pentecost celebrations, rose petals would be let down through the holes in the roof by some brave parishioner willing to ascend there and await a cue, the petals falling down upon worshippers as a reminder of the tongues of fire that came to rest upon the early followers of Jesus.[4] Doves, likewise, would be let loose down through the holes at just the right time in the liturgy to fly around the sanctuary, another enlivening

---

4. Acts 2:1–4.

reminder of how the Spirit lives and moves freely in our midst.[5] If the Holy Spirit of God cannot be manipulated, controlled, or contained, we would do well to remember that our reading of the Bible likewise ought to be characterized not only by holiness but also by holeness. Openness to the Spirit through the text. Openness to interpretation. Freedom to read both into and out of the text, as we all do anyway, even if we're not always ready to admit that. That doesn't mean that any and every reading of the Bible is valid. It does mean recognizing, however, that the ways the Holy Spirit may touch our lives through the biblical text transcend only one or two narrow meanings. To read the Bible apart from an invitation for the Holy Spirit to speak intimately and freely to our hearts there is akin to reading dead words on a slice of dead tree. But to read Scripture with the prayerful expectation and invitation for God the Holy Spirit to burst into and blow through our lives all over again, like at Pentecost, this is to read Scripture in a way that raptures our hearts, enlivens our spirits, and pierces with passion the mind that yearns to know the living God truly and deeply. To engage the Bible in this life-giving way one simply must be willing to wonder, to wonder with the Spirit and the text together, and to wonder about what is absent from the text as much as about what is present in the text.

The poor widow who places two coins in the temple treasury, Jesus says, offers more than all the rich who have contributed combined. Jesus comments, "All these people gave their gifts out of their wealth; but she out of her poverty put in all she had to live on."[6] What good words and what a great story. I can picture Jesus hanging out by the temple, observing the people giving, *how* they're giving, how *much* they're giving, *what* they're giving, and then, suddenly, this woman catches Jesus' eye. And if something catches Jesus' eye, it doubly warrants our time and attention. Notice in the story how this most remarkable demonstration of generosity is marked at its core by anonymity. The poor widow's name is absent. We never learn who she is. Attention is drawn to the

5. Eck, *Encountering God*, 130.

6. Luke 21:4

act of giving rather than to the *ego* behind the giving. Who she is remains a cipher. What might this absence have to teach us about the widow's offering and our offerings in general?

Zechariah and his wife Elizabeth are visited by an angel who announces they will have a baby. This baby will grow up to become John the Baptist, cousin to Jesus and the one who will prepare the way of the Lord. But Zechariah doubts this good news. Who can blame him? Sometimes good news, even at times more than bad news, is overwhelming and bewildering. As a result of his disbelief, Zechariah is thrust into a period of silence, not for 9 days, not for 9 weeks, but for no less than 9 months. Remarkable! Remarkable, that is, if we take the story seriously, and why shouldn't we. It's not until eight days after the birth of baby John that finally Zechariah's tongue is loosed. Can you imagine what was going through Zechariah's mind for all those months when he found himself absent the ability to speak? What thoughts were gestating quietly inside him? What becomes of our thoughts and the stirrings in our hearts when we allow ourselves to enter into silence?

I wonder about Abraham's silence, too, going back to Genesis 22. There is a remarkable absence in Scripture here, famously known as "the Silence of Abraham," a silence that takes place in between what God says to Abraham in verse 2 and what Abraham begins to do in verse 3. God calls out to Abraham and says in verse 2: "Take your son, your only son, whom you love—Isaac—and go to the region of Moriah. Sacrifice him there as a burnt offering on a mountain I will show you."[7] Abraham's response is seen in verse 3: "Early the next morning Abraham got up and loaded his donkey. He took with him two of his servants and his son Isaac. When he had cut enough wood for the burnt offering, he set out for the place God had told him about."[8]

Did you catch it? The absence in between verse 2 and verse 3? We need to read carefully, and to proceed tenderly, not too quickly, to notice these "Holy Spirit holes" in the text. The spaces in between are precious. God asks Abraham in verse 2 to kill his

7. Gen 22:2.
8. Gen 22:3.

son, his one and only son whom he loves, and in verse 3 Abraham responds how? Abraham's response is *silent obedience*. How outrageous! What was going through Abraham's mind? What would be going through your mind? If I am really open to the possibility of this story, entering into Abraham's shoes for even a few moments, I have to imagine that if *God* were asking *me* to sacrifice my son Joshua or my daughter Bella, even with that request coming from God, I have to imagine that my response would be protest, fury, angry denial, kicking and screaming and running in the other direction, just about anything and everything *except* silent obedience! Yet it is precisely this absence—the silence of Abraham—that invites us deeper into the text and deeper into ourselves and the Spirit to reflect on what faith really means vis-à-vis such a radically other God who would ask such a thing. Abraham gives us no verbal cue as to what was going on in his heart and head regarding the God who had called him to such an act. It's this absence in the story, insipid, and tacit, that is ripe for reflection and a catalyst for our self-transformation.

How do you read the Bible? Some churches emphasize, even overemphasize, the literal aspects of the Bible, the words verbatim on the page, the historical facts behind what is written on the page, memorizing what is written on the page, and so on and so forth. There are good aspects to this to be sure. I encourage our family, for example, to commit to memory just a single Bible verse a month as one way for us to stay spiritually rooted, healthy, and strong.

But the literal can only take us so far. The Bible is a spiritual book intended for spiritual use. It's a book of faith written by people of faith. More than that, as John Calvin believed, as do I, the Bible is meant to help us transcend the words on its pages in order to connect us with the living Word.[9] That's what really matters. The Bible is not primarily a history book, though it contains plenty of history. The Bible is not essentially a science book, nor was it ever meant to be taken as a science *textbook* as some have come to do. The Bible has always been treated by people of faith as first and

9. Calvin, *Institutes of the Christian Religion*, 74–92.

foremost a spiritual text, meant for enriching the lives of people living in the Spirit. If we keep this simple truth in mind when we read its pages, whether with our families or congregations or individually, we will open ourselves to something wonderful and exhilarating: the living God. Never contained. Always free to rearrange (us) by helping us to engage the text, especially in wonder, paying attention to what's there, but also to what's not. This inquisitive, probing, childlike approach to the Bible is what we might call (to borrow a phrase from Saint Anselm) *fides quaerens intellectum*. This approach does not presume that we have all the answers, nor does it read the Bible primarily as an answer book, but rather engages the Bible humbly as a way of "faith seeking understanding."

21

BLACK

Black is the absence of light. It is the darkest color. Black is beautiful. It was one of the first colors used in cave paintings dating back more than ten thousand years ago. Black is also rich with symbolic overtones of that which is stark, hard, and disquieting. In this way each of us is familiar with that which is black.

In the Bible the Psalmist at one point shares words that no doubt anyone can relate to at one time or another: "I am overwhelmed with troubles . . . . You have put me in the lowest pit, in the darkest depths."[1] Who hasn't felt like they've been put in a bad spot overwhelmed with troubles? Who hasn't at times felt like the light of life has been eclipsed—for whatever reason—like life is a pit suffused in darkness? This is part of the human experience and it can happen with or without identifiable reasons, like divorce, or a sudden death in the family, catching us off guard. We can surprisingly find ourselves feeling weary, worn, heavy-hearted, and without always knowing the impetus behind these feelings that come to steal away the light and levity of life, replacing them with a shroud of pitch black.

---

1. Ps 88:3, 6.

It is remarkable, even startling, that the Psalmist identifies God as the one who has put him or her in the darkest depths of the pit. Yet there is ambiguity for the Psalmist on this point. God is identified in the text as the one who saves *and* as the source of darkness.[2] Both. At the heart of this ambiguity the Psalmist has many questions, as do we, not the least of which is whether or not God's wonders can be known in the black oblivion of life's bleak moments.[3] The questions are left unanswered. There is the absence of an answer, perhaps precisely because there are no convenient solutions or easy answers when you're in the pit, though Scripture does invite us like the Psalmist to engage the dark ambiguity of the pit for ourselves. Engaging it, even without attempting a resolution, is different than just leaving the ambiguity "there" as a nuisance. When we're in the blackness of the pit, unable to see or get our bearings, we tend to believe this space is nothing but bad, perhaps because it *feels* bad. But that's not the whole story, and the Psalmist in effect says just this, that our suffering, and the God who saves, are not separate but rather, somehow, intertwined.

Too often we think when bad things happen to us it is due to our own bad choices, or to the forces and accidents of nature, or in extreme cases of suffering we may even attribute such evil to an evil one, the Devil. But the notion that God might actually be right in the middle of our darkest moments is something that doesn't often occur to us, at least not at first. Surely we must be cautious never to attempt to comfort others in the midst of a tragedy with the heinous notion that it's all just part of God's plan. This is hardly comforting, or true, even if the Psalmist at times leans heavily in this direction. Such shallow theology too often only serves to intensify the pain and to turn too many away from a God who would seemingly cause cancer, car wrecks, and other catastrophes. Yet there is a world of difference between saying straightforwardly God caused my tragedy and saying as the Psalmist does with confusion, complexity, questions, nuance, and ambivalence that the

2. Ps 88:1, 18.
3. Ps 88:10–14.

God who saves is likewise the God who is somehow hidden with me even in the depths of the pit.

Is God with us in the black? I think so. Isn't that what we see in Jesus? That God is with us even and especially in our cruciform moments? That God so loved us that God was willing to enter the messiness of human existence even with all of its pain and suffering? That God was even willing to suffer the darkness of death in order to grace us once again with the gift of life? Jesus, far from being some otherworldly figure untouched by the real troubles of real life, in truth, was very much a man of sorrows quite familiar with the black. His illumination was revealed to us not apart from but rather in, with, and through the black.[4]

The renowned twentieth century psychologist Carl Jung understood the nature of life itself this way. Jung experienced his own pit, like the Psalmist, like Jesus the suffering servant, when from 1913 to 1922 he underwent a traumatic break with his mentor Sigmund Freud. This break was immediately followed by the death of his mother, and saturated by the horrors of the First World War. What Jung eventually came to see during this bleak time is something that words fail to sufficiently convey and only one's own experience can know the potency of: *there is no resurrection without crucifixion.* There is no spring without winter. There is no ascending without descending. That is to say, so often the new beginnings we yearn for cannot be realized apart from the threshold space of first enduring pitch-black, womb-like, tomb-like darkness.

A good number of truly special people throughout history have recognized this truth as well; Jung is not alone.[5] Beethoven in 1787 when he was just sixteen years old revealed a defining feature about his life that would remain a constant right up to the very end. In a letter written soon after the death of his beloved mother, he confesses he has been suffering from grief, from asthma, and also from one other thing: melancholy. Over the next several years, not despite this, but more so because of this, Beethoven goes on

---

4. Isa 50:4–9, 52:13—53:12.

5. I am indebted here to Eric G. Wilson, *Against Happiness*, 49–77, 123–25.

to produce several remarkable pieces including his Moonlight Sonata. In a letter to a physician friend in 1801 he points to his muse. He writes with characteristic intensity saying, on the one hand, he is quite pleased with everything. He enjoys his work. His compositions are selling easily. He has few financial concerns. Yet he plainly admits at the same time he is prone to giving way to full-out despair. He confesses that both the light and darkness engulf his life and, strangely, there seems to be a place for both. Beethoven sees that as much as he dislikes the melancholy, when he finds himself in it, he embraces it, because it helps to give rise to his great work, that it is undesirable and yet also a creative force, an ironic energy of inspiration.

A few centuries before Beethoven, the Renaissance philosopher Marsilio Ficino discovered the same. Ficino writes that for as long as he can remember he's been quite content, but that he's also quite easily given to melancholia. As he nears the end of his life he confesses he is downright tired of these black spells. The constant up and down of life feels exhausting. So, he wonders if perhaps he has been misled for far too long about the dark aspects of his being. Is there a more positive way to understand this dimension of his life, since it seems to be an unavoidable part of life? He admits that often he has sought to escape the pit when he finds himself in its depths, usually by sticking his head in a book (Ficino was a translator of the works of Plato and found great pleasure in reading), and that perhaps such occasional escapism isn't all bad. But he reasons such escapism can't be all good either. He thinks there must be something more to the non-happy seasons of life than always just trying to "get through" them or avoiding them. Eventually, while reading a passage from Aristotle, Ficino has an epiphany. Aristotle writes: "Why is it that all those who have become eminent in philosophy or politics or poetry or in the arts are clearly melancholics?" As Ficino broods over these words he begins to glimpse a dawn, namely, that melancholy, too, has a time and a place in our lives. The pit has a place. Black has a place on the palette of life. Ficino goes on to write a groundbreaking work called *The Book of Life* in which he shows melancholia to be a catalyst for the creative spirit. Without the black of melancholy, Ficino says, we simply wouldn't have many of the great works of art, literature, music, and more that we do today.

This is an encouraging word to any of us learning to be with the black in life. Darkness has a place, a catalytic place. Joy and sorrow are never separated, nor very far from one another. Henri Nouwen observes that "when our hearts rejoice at a spectacular view, we may miss our friends who cannot see it, and when we are overwhelmed with grief, we may discover what true friendship is all about. Joy is hidden in sorrow and sorrow in joy. If we try to avoid sorrow at all costs, we may never taste joy, and if we are suspicious of ecstasy, agony can never reach us either."[6] Even if we'd prefer it otherwise, joy *and* sorrow are the parents of our spiritual growth.

6. Nouwen, *Bread for the Journey*, 2.

22

COMING AND GOING WITH NOTHING

One of the things I love about the Bible is its frequent use of candor. No beating around the bush. Just the truth plain and simple in all of its shocking splendor. We see such straightforwardness in the Message translation of the following words about our entrance and departure from this world in Ecclesiastes: We are born with nothing, and we die with nothing. Nothing is our inheritance, and nothing is our sum total. So why bother working so hard for a salary of smoke?[1]

It's true. We witness this all the time. People rushing around busy with a million different things, working so hard for this and for that, and for what, really? The Bible reminds us our coming into this world and our going from this world is marked by nothing. We arrive absolutely naked and with absolutely nothing less and nothing more than who we are. When we depart, it's not just our belongings that disappear from us. Indeed, our very presence in this world moves decidedly into absence. Yet, despite this stark reality, we seem so often to turn a blind eye to the truth of our coming and going. We either fear or don't know what to do with the nothingness that hedges us in on every side smirking at the

1. Eccl 5:16–17.

house of cards we feverishly continue to build as if it were something more than that. This is not to say that all our labor in life is in vain.[2] Yet time for too many of us is time to *spend*, time to *acquire*, time to do nothing more than *do, do, do* before our time runs out.

The Celtic imagination held a different conception, and experience, of time. Beyond doing, time was also time for wonder. Against the rapidity and incessantly purpose-driven sensibilities of our day and age, time for the Celts of ancient Ireland was approached with a gracious inquisitiveness. There was time to behold and reacquaint oneself with the forgotten mystery in the world and in oneself. There is a delightful story about a hectic man traveling through a twisted jungle with several native guides.[3] This man was in a desperate hurry. They all raced onward, driven by his agenda, without stopping for three days straight. At the end of the third day, the natives leading the busy man sat down and would not move. The man urged them to get up. He told them of the pressure he was under to reach his destination before a certain date. But they refused. He could not understand their refusal. After much pleading, they still refused to move. Finally, he was able to persuade one of them to share the reason for their pausing. The native said, "We have moved too quickly to reach here; now we need to wait to give our spirits a chance to catch up with us."

Many people who are secretly weary of life have left little space for time: time to wonder, time to be away from work, time for their spirits to catch up with them. They have decidedly, or accidentally, filled the emptiness. They are tacitly or explicitly obsessed with an agenda. These agendas are typically rationalized and buttressed by very noble reasons and religious people are certainly not exempt from this common malady. "Build the kingdom!" "Advance the organization!" "Sell the product!" I'm reminded of something Thomas Merton once said: "There are some men for whom a tree has no reality until they think of cutting it down . . . ."[4] How sad. To

---

2. Ps 127:1.

3. O'Donohue, *Anam Cara*, 151–52.

4. Merton, *No Man Is an Island*, 258.

be obsessed with utility and building the future eclipses the gift of the present and the beauty of what is right before us.

While living in Massachusetts for a time, I knew a great woman of faith in her mid-nineties. Sylvia, in the twilight of life, was a rugged woman with fierce resolve who had accomplished much. But it seemed her final years had brought a new softness to her ways, a deeper appreciation for the truth that she would soon be going from this life with nothing, just as she had come into this life with nothing. I had the rare opportunity one afternoon a few months before her passing to ask a rather candid question: "What have you learned in life?" I probed knowing she would thoroughly enjoy the question. "What's most important?" Our elders so often have tender wisdom we fail to receive or forget to even ask for. Sylvia looked out the window for a moment before looking me straight in the eye with her reply: "Don't worry. Don't worry so much about doing so much. Take time to be happy," she said emphatically. I smiled at the wisdom of her reply as I thought of Aristotle who taught that the highest good of human existence is *eudaemonia* (flourishing/happiness) and Bobby McFerrin who encouraged us melodically in the nineties with the cheerful adage "don't worry, be happy." Sylvia died not long after what turned out to be our final conversation. Presiding at her funeral a few weeks later these lovely words from Jesus found a most fitting place and are worth quoting at length:

> "Therefore I tell you, do not worry about your life, what you will eat or drink; or about your body, what you will wear. Is not life more than food, and the body more than clothes? Look at the birds of the air; they do not sow or reap or store away in barns, and yet your heavenly Father feeds them. Are you not much more valuable than they? Can any one of you by worrying add a single hour to your life? And why do you worry about clothes? See how the flowers of the field grow. They do not labor or spin.

Yet I tell you that not even Solomon in all his splendor was dressed like one of these. If that is how God clothes the grass of the field, which is here today and tomorrow is thrown into the fire, will he not much more clothe you—you of little faith? So do not worry, saying, 'What shall we eat?' or 'What shall we drink?' or 'What shall we wear?' For the pagans run after all these things, and your heavenly Father knows that you need them. But seek first his kingdom and his righteousness, and all these things will be given to you as well. Therefore do not worry about tomorrow, for tomorrow will worry about itself. Each day has enough trouble of its own."[5]

It is no small thing that Jesus encourages us not to worry. Jesus, living at the time of his ministry within an apocalyptic worldview characterized by the imminent expectation of a dramatic and dastardly end to all things, could have very easily been worried about many things. Jesus could have also been worried about his own end, for it seems quite likely he knew his teachings and actions would bring about a dangerous demise to his own coming and going. Jesus could have even religiously rationalized being worried, frantically hurrying about to share his message and to advance God's kingdom here on earth.

By contrast, we witness Jesus taking plenty of time to enjoy meals with friends, and even the marginalized of society. Taking time to talk with strangers and with little children. Taking time early in the day to commune in the quiet with his Lord. Jesus models time to wonder: about life, God, and what really matters. Jesus models time to be: with others and with God. It's good not only to practice what you preach but also to preach what you practice, and here in this passage from Matthew 6 we see Jesus verbally affirming what he so clearly already lived in his life.

"Why," we might wonder, "did the Son of God have this relaxed attitude and posture toward life?" The answer appears in the midst of his discourse here in Matthew 6 and is twofold. First, we don't need to worry because God *is* for us.[6] But, secondly, there's

5. Matt 6:25–34.
6. Matt 6:26, 30.

no sense in fretting about the future because each day has enough trouble of its own.[7] How true! Jesus didn't look at life through rose-colored glasses. He knew full well that life is difficult. Yet, his trust in the graciousness of God was greater. His faith set him free from worry and from what he deemed a pagan preoccupation with running after many things.[8] His faith situated his attention profoundly in the present. Jesus had time, indeed *made* time, for the gift of being, here, now.

7. Matt 6:34.
8. Matt 6:32.

23

NOTHING TO DO

"There's nothing to do!" my kids complained the other day, "We're bored!" The announcement came no more than a few minutes on the heels of an exciting movie we had just finished watching, swimming at the pool the day prior, as well as having recently returned from a delightful vacation with our family in Connecticut. All I could do was smile at Isabella and Joshua in amusement.

Yet we, too, as adults, despite our busyness, are far from impervious to the specter of boredom. Most of us who are honest enough will plainly admit that boredom *does* come knocking on our doors, time and time again, stealth-like in its approach, slipping in between the cracks and spaces that separate our many activities. It doesn't seem to matter how much we have on our plates. The absence of anything to do, or rather the unwavering feeling and perception that there is nothing to do, is a structural feature of being a human being. It creeps up on all of us. While we cannot erase its existence, we can come to see how very useful, and even surprisingly illuminating, the nothingness of boredom actually is.

Many great thinkers have given their attention to the phenomenon of boredom throughout the centuries, believe it or not. Our experience of "empty time" matters.[1] The conundrum of the draining sense that there is nothing to do is more significant than at first glance. Soren Kierkegaard brought his mental prowess to it in the nineteenth century, and John Cassian before him in the fourth and fifth century. But one of my favorite readings on the meaning of boredom comes from the Russian poet and essayist Joseph Brodsky who was awarded the Nobel Prize in Literature in 1987 and had this to say, curiously, in praise of boredom: "When hit by boredom, go for it. Let yourself be crushed by it; submerge, hit bottom. . . . The reason boredom deserves such scrutiny is that it represents pure, undiluted time in all its repetitive, redundant, monotonous splendor."[2]

Why would Brodsky dare such audacious words? Because they are true. No doubt it has a strange ring to our ears at first. Boredom? Something for us to sit and be with? At least more so than we are often willing? Boredom, also known under the aliases of tedium, doldrums, ennui, anguish, and acedia, is a complex phenomenon, though by and large the child of nothing other than plain repetition. And what is life if not an endless series of repetitions? Repetition of course has its place, even a positive one at that, as when a woman practices again and again the scales on her musical instrument so as to make melodious sounds, or when a man repeatedly works the routines of a kata in the martial arts in order to become proficient in self-defense. But children will be all too quick to remind us of the darker and duller side of repetition. Why do I have to make my bed when I'm just going to sleep in it again? Why do I have to clean my room when it's just going to get messy again? Though we typically dismiss such questions, these are actually penetrating questions that quickly cut to the heart of one of life's central dilemmas: *the absence of anything new under*

1. Raposa, *Boredom and the Religious Imagination*, 4, 42–44.
2. Brodsky, *On Grief and Reason*, 108–9.

the sun produces the sensation of boredom. It's unavoidable. Life's main medium is precisely repetition; anything displaying a pattern is already at the very least pregnant with boredom.[3]

Still we try to avoid boredom in any variety of ways. But whatever our method of escape, our reasons are not so different. "In general, a man shooting heroin into his vein does so largely for the same reason you buy a video: to dodge the redundancy of time."[4] Reading a book by E. L. James. Taking up a hobby. Playing Super Mario Brothers. Betting at the racetrack. Our forms of escapism may differ; the reasons not so much.

But if life's repetitions tend to give way to the feeble pain of boredom, we can nevertheless trust this pain as the poet W. H. Auden once said, whom Joseph Brodsky was fond of quoting:

> "But should you fail to keep your kingdom
> And, like your father before you, come
> Where thought accuses and feeling mocks,
> Believe your pain . . ."[5]

Pain doesn't lie. Not the pain of loss or heartache or boredom. "Believe your pain." That is to say, *there is truth even in the pain of boredom.* And truth, as Jesus taught, however uncomfortable at times, is always worth receiving, because it is the truth that has the power to set us free.[6] Brodsky goes so far as to say, and I am fully inclined to agree with him here, that the truth of the nothingness of boredom can actually lead us to become more humble, and more compassionate. How? By realizing that we are all caught up in the repetitiveness of life—and that's okay. Knowing this puts us in our place. Even more than that, we learn that we can hold each other, gently, and honestly, even in life's banal moments.

The next time you feel like there's nothing to do, I implore you, don't rush past it. Don't rush to fill the void, too quickly, though no

3. Ibid., 104–5.

4. Ibid., 107.

5. Auden, *The Sea and the Mirror*, 21.

6. John 8:32. This is my third time referencing this particular Scripture. I do so with good reason. These are some of Jesus' most profound words to us: the truth *does* have the power to set us free.

doubt you eventually will and eventually that's okay. Distractions have a place. First, however, *savor what is*. There *is* nothing new under the sun; what has been will be again.[7] If Jesus is right and I trust he is—"the truth will set you free"—then the truth of life's boring moments has so very much to offer you! Accept it into your bosom! As much as you can for I know it's hard. But whoever said that life was going to be easy, though we continually imagine that it ought to be. "Life is difficult . . . ." These are the very first three words of M. Scott Peck's famous book *The Road Less Traveled*. They stand out. They are reminiscent of the Buddha's teaching that life is suffering as well as Jesus' promise that in this world you *will* have trouble. A road less traveled that we do well to take is the one that doesn't skirt but rather embraces the strange and hidden blessing of boredom. Though it is easier to ignore, there is something for us in the nothing. We should remember that easy ways do not come from God.[8]

A disciple once asked his master, "What does one need in order to be fully Awake?" The master replied, "You must discover what it is that falls in the water and does not make a ripple; moves through the trees and does not make a sound; enters the field and does not stir a single blade of grass." After weeks of fruitless pondering, the disciple asked, "What is this thing?" "Thing?" said the master. "It isn't a thing at all." "So it is nothing?" the disciple asked. The master replied, "You might say so."[9]

If God is No-thing—for all *things* are created, and God is the Creator, not the created—then nothing is as close to what we can say we are truly searching for in our journey of "waking up."[10] The nothingness of boredom has its place.

---

7. Eccl 1:9.

8. Merton, *The Way of Chuang Tzu*, 52.

9. De Mello, *Awakening*, 12.

10. Eph 5:14.

24

SACRIFICE

The notion of giving up something for another appeals to that which is noble in our nature. We like the idea of sacrifice. Yet the practice of making a sacrifice is an entirely different matter.

Too often we flounder the moment we begin to bridge the gap between idea and praxis, notion and reality. I have a friend in the ministry living in Nigeria dealing with Boko Haram and dire needs, and another friend who travels through Syria regularly as a missionary faced with the very real threat of car bombings and the like. I always feel humbled after having been in their presence. What sacrifices do we here in the states typically face? Let's be honest, we struggle giving up a few extra minutes to allow another car out in front of us in a long, long line of traffic we've been sitting in impatiently. We struggle giving up a Saturday to cover for a co-worker so she doesn't have to miss her daughter's dance recital. Our list of "sacrifices" goes on and on. Contentment and discontentment. Gladness and resistance. Both so often mark even our smallest sacrificial acts. As twenty-first century North Americans so very many of us have much to learn about the meaning of that which is arguably the very centerpiece of Jesus' life: sacrifice.

The Bible tells us to present ourselves as a living sacrifice to God. It says when we live sacrificially this is worship.[1] Worship is not going to church once a week or praying or singing songs—not in the first instance, not in the biblical view. Worship is quintessentially about living for others and the Other. It's about giving. It's about giving yourself to God and those whom God calls you to love. Sacrifice is the worshipful act of living generously. *Being* giving. As opposed to simply doing a nice thing here or there to appease our conscience or show ourselves good to others. Living sacrificially is a vital understanding of the nature of worship because it moves us beyond Sundays and occasional charity and anchors the reality of loving God in a daily rhythm of being more and more for others and more and more for God systemically.

The systemic nature of sacrifice is far more radical than we typically realize at first. By choosing any set of specific responsibilities, such as giving yourself to one profession or one way of service over another, we by default sacrifice our duties to billions of *other* human beings who also have claims on us.[2] To devote yourself to your family, as a stay-at-home mother does, for example, is by default to absent yourself from other duties to your community and nation. To devote yourself to your nation, as a newly enlisted young man or woman does in the Navy, for example, is likewise by default to absent yourself from other duties to your family. That is to say, sacrifice is inescapable. Though we typically don't realize it, we cannot get away from it, even if we wanted to. Sacrifice is a decision only in part. In truth, sacrifice is less a decision and more a pervasive reality we *already* find ourselves immersed in etched in every decision we make. This is ironic because most of the time we think of making a sacrifice for another as an uninhibited choice. But that's only because we are unaware of how *any and every choice* simultaneously absents us from other choices, the *de facto* creation of sacrifice. The philosopher Jacques Derrida got it right when he said that sacrifice, actually, is the most common event in the

---

1. Rom 12:1.

2. Cosgrove, *The Meanings We Choose*, 18.

world.[3] "Everyone is being sacrificed to everyone else in this land of Moriah," says Derrida, "our habitat every second of every day."[4]

The land of Moriah that Derrida refers to is an allusion to Genesis 22 where Abraham binds his very own son, Isaac, in preparation for sacrifice. The Bible here dilutes our lofty, self-righteous notions of sacrifice, soberly reminding us of its simple grim nature: sacrifice hurts. It hurt Jesus to love us on the cross. It hurt Abraham to follow the will of God for his son Isaac, though Isaac ultimately was spared. Yes, there is also joy in giving. But we blind ourselves sentimentally and unnecessarily if we obscure the pain that is part and parcel of living sacrificially. We might think about it like this: you are going to suffer any which way in this life. That's life. But *how* will you suffer? Will your suffering be by happenstance, simply as a part of existence, or will your pain constitute something more, for others, and even for Another?

Sacrifice is not optional for any of us. To choose one thing is simultaneously to sacrifice something else. In Genesis 22, if we don't presume to know the safe outcome for Isaac—which Abraham did not know ahead of time—we see that if Abraham sacrifices Isaac, he goes with the will of God, but loses his son. If Abraham sacrifices the will of God, he forsakes his heavenly Father, yet remains a father to his son.

Sacrifice is unavoidable in this land of Moriah for us, too, not only for Abraham. Sacrifice is woven into the fabric of life, happening by default every moment we choose one path, any path, over another to give ourselves to. So be discerning. Choose with care your *form* of sacrifice. It is an unavoidable choice. As God once said to the Hebrew people long ago, "This day I call the heavens and the earth as witnesses against you that I have set before you life and death, blessings and curses. Now choose life, so that you and your children may live and that you may love the Lord your God, listen to his voice, and hold fast to him. For the Lord is your life . . . ."[5]

3. Derrida, *The Gift of Death*, 69.

4. Ibid., 69.

5. Deut 30:19–20.

Sacrifice is very much about recognizing the duality of what we choose, how each choice forces the absence of something else. If a woman chooses to spend her paycheck frivolously each week on immediate pleasures, eating out and buying new clothes and the acquisition of the latest pocket technology, to her heart's content, she is also choosing the absence of a secure financial future, and sacrificing more generous ends for her money. But this is the reality for all of us! For you. For me. For all our sacrifices.

Sacrifice is about seeing: when you choose one thing, you also choose the absence of another. The addition of all our sacrifices, the world over, creates a ripple effect that shapes our world for better or worse. It is a lie to believe destiny lies anywhere else than in our own hands.

Jesus said something significant about sacrifice when teaching his followers, vividly and hyperbolically, if your right eye causes you to stumble, gouge it out and throw it away. He went on to say that if your right hand causes you to stumble, likewise, cut it off and throw it out. Jesus says it is wise to sacrifice parts, rather than the whole, in order to preserve the integrity of the whole.[6] Jesus' words here are not meant to be taken literally (as Origen did in the third century which led to an unfortunate self-castration). However, they are meant to be taken seriously. Jesus' words convey a strong note of realism. We may very well have to "lop off" certain parts of ourselves, lifestyles, habits, attitudes, and more if we want to see our world flourish. Growth is hard. It hurts. It involves pruning. Living sacrificially is committing to a vibrant way, Jesus' way, but such giving, letting go, and even lopping off implies change, and change is the textbook definition of that which is difficult. W. H. Auden once said:

> "We would rather be ruined than change,
> We would rather die in our dread
> Than climb the cross of the moment
> And let our illusions die."[7]

---

6. Matt 5:29–30.

7. Auden, *The Age of Anxiety*, 105.

Yet let our illusions die we must. We cannot escape the all-embracing sea of sacrifice.

Living sacrificially is the way of Jesus. We can rest assured that to follow in his footsteps is to approach daily divine shores. When Jesus asked his followers to "repent" (*metanoia* in the New Testament Greek) because the kingdom of God has come near, what he literally told them to do was "change."[8] Change, in other words, is not only difficult. It is also a gift. Change connects us with the kingdom.

Change is one of the gifts that has kept my heart anchored to the church for as many years as I've been in it because despite the sacrifices that are part and parcel of the pastorate I cannot deny how my heart skips a beat in love and adoration every time I witness God changing another person's life. *Metanoia* happens. Change *is* possible. Jesus would not have called any of us to do something he considered improbable or impossible. Jesus had a tremendous amount of faith not only in God but also in us. We *can* change. And the first steps in that direction are often sacrifices (well chosen).

Living sacrificially can mean letting go of a critical way of engaging others, or yourself, in conversation or self-talk. We might need to lop off an overly judgmental way of looking at those who believe or behave differently from us. Some of us need to re-examine our monthly budgets to see if our giving is really in alignment with our priorities and God's priority for the poor. Sometimes we need to forgive another, or forgive ourselves, for life not turning out as we had hoped, so that we can live into the bright future God has in store for us now. Sometimes, however, sacrificial living needs to begin more basically at home. Upon receiving the Nobel Peace Prize, Mother Teresa was asked what we could do to promote world peace. What a gigantic question. She answered, simply and directly, "Go home, and love your family."

You are one person, graced with one life, a finite amount of time, by an infinitely gracious God who is longing each day for you to live passionately, which means like Jesus living sacrificially.

---

8. Matt 4:17.

This is your true act of daily worship. Well chosen "Yeses" but also well chosen "Nos."[9] Know where to put your presence, and your absence.

9. Matt 5:37.

25

NATURE ABHORS A VACUUM

Emptiness cannot sustain itself and in a sense longs to be filled with something. Nature abhors a vacuum. This principle is sometimes referred to in physics as first proposed by Aristotle as the *horror vacui*. It seems doubtful that there is anything like strict nothingness, absolute absence, or entire emptiness in the universe. The deepest freeze, as we understand it, for example, in the very basements of space, is around 2.7 degrees above so-called absolute zero, signaling the presence there of *something* in motion. Even a vacuum empty of all matter is still an ocean of energy in the form of fluctuating electromagnetic waves, as shown by their exerting a force on uncharged plates (a prediction made by Dutch physicist Hendrick Casimir in 1948 and finally confirmed in 1996 at Los Alamos).[1] This is known as "vacuum energy," indicating that a vacuum isn't really a vacuum at all but rather is ripe with infinite energy, at least according to current theory. Even air is *something*, despite appearances, filled with electrons, protons, quarks, and the like.[2] The discovery of supermassive black holes being a commonplace in the universe, contrary to initial predications of their

1. Kaplan, *The Nothing That Is*, 177–78.
2. Close, *Nothing*, 7.

oddity and rarity, wherein the very laws of physics are crushed out of existence, may be the last threshold for the possibility of the discovery of real nothingness. But for now, from what we know of the physical world, both on a macroscopic and microscopic level, emptiness in our lives is more of a feeling, an experience, and an idea—and an extremely useful one at that. Think again of our friend zero. Where would we be in mathematics without zero? Without the zero hour of midnight to start a new day? Without a prime meridian to make our maps? Without the zero point on our thermometers? The *idea* of the empty is crucial and ideas are never "just" ideas. Ideas have legs as the philosopher Francis Schaeffer once pointed out. Indeed, countless creations of mankind had their beginnings as ideas incubating in the mind before they became incarnate. Ideas are powerful. In spirituality, the idea of emptiness is most important for living, not theorizing.

To that end, for the next few moments, I would suggest trying this exercise from the beloved David Kundtz.[3] Resist the temptation to read on right now. Instead, pause. Pause, be empty, and sink into *each* of the movements here:

Be still ...
Breathe ...
Relax ...
Breathe again ...
And again ...
Let a little time pass, doing nothing ...

The fourteenth century mystic Meister Eckhart taught "God is not found in the soul by adding anything but by a process of subtraction."[4] Your well-being hinges not on adding more to your life but rather the opposite: subtracting more. Less is more. Emptying can be restorative.

I experienced this just the other day as I was sitting down for lunch on a park bench to enjoy a most delicious ham and sharp cheddar cheese sandwich with honey mustard dressing on a fresh

3. Kundtz, *Moments In Between*, 43.
4. Eckhart, *Selected Treatises and Sermons*, 167.

sourdough baguette. It was exquisite. Before I took my first bite and just after I prayed giving thanks for the food, I took a few moments to practice exactly what you just practiced—doing nothing, being empty. Then, as I began to enjoy my lunch no more than a minute or so after having done nothing, a complete stranger went out of her way to walk over to where I was seated. "You are the calmest person I've seen today," she said. I was surprised by the encounter yet that is exactly how I felt. Calm. Refreshed.

I share this not as self-aggrandizement but to highlight the gravity of what the Bible teaches, beyond mere words, when it says, "Be still, and know that I am God."[5] This is so *very* important for our soul-health. We can read these biblical words a hundred times and still not understand their meaning. That's because understanding in this case comes from practicing. Ruminating is not enough. *Practicing* emptiness is important because it creates receptive space within: space for receiving and knowing God.

Yet anyone who has ever tried through prayer or meditation to relax and empty the mind, to enjoy what the Japanese call *mushin* ("no mind"), is all too familiar with how easily the mind is flooded with thought after thought after thought. Again, nature seems to abhor a vacuum. Even beyond prayer and meditation we are quite familiar with the frustrations of the mind as we lie awake at night, on our drive home from work, indeed in just about every capacity one can imagine in life.

There are two spiritually useful ways for dealing with the mind's cantankerousness. First, in meditation and prayer, we should remember that the practice of emptying the mind is not a subtle attempt to frustrate us by drawing our attention to the continual onslaught of random distracting thoughts, though it might feel that way at times. Instead, those who mindfully seek to make space for God inwardly should imagine our troubling and distracting thoughts as nothing more than clouds, easily and gently passing out of the mind as easily as they come in. This gentle imagery helps to still the mind.

5. Ps 46:10.

Second, we can bring stillness to the mind by remembering that emptiness is sometimes gateway to a greater end. Emptiness is not always an end in itself. It can have purpose. Pascal wrote that there is a God-shaped vacuum in the heart of every person which cannot be filled by any created thing, but only by God.[6] Nature abhors a vacuum—even in the human mind—and thus the practice of emptying the mind of random, bad, and distracting thoughts is not necessarily to leave the mind empty but rather to make room inwardly so that we can be more receptive of God, and the lovely things God desires to share with us. If we learn anything from the incarnation of the Christ in the New Testament it is that God wants to fill us, to permeate our minds and hearts. You are God's beloved. God yearns to fill you to overflowing. Practicing stillness, providing receptive space for God throughout each day, can be such a blessing. The monk Evagrius taught, "the practice of stillness is full of joy and beauty."[7]

Not long after my spiritual awakening, which dawned during the end of my teenage years, I received a word from the Lord, something like an impassioned love letter, in non-textual form, about the person I was to become. Though it had not been my plan or intent I discovered I was to be a teacher. That discovery, surprising as it was to someone who had been making preparations to enter the film industry, came to me as I began practicing more stillness. For the first time in my life, as I sought real and regular attentiveness, inwardly, to God, I began to "hear" more of that still, small voice the Bible speaks to us about. This passage from Isaiah has held special meaning for me ever since: "The Lord God has given me the tongue of a teacher, that I may know how to sustain the weary with a word. Morning by morning he wakens—wakens my ear to listen as those who are taught."[8] Both my father and mother were teachers before me and it seems the calling on my life has been to become a teacher of sorts as well. But one cannot properly "teach" anyone anything, spiritual or otherwise,

6. Pascal, *Pensées*, 75.

7. Laird, *A Sunlit Absence*, 9.

8. Isa 50:4.

unless you are first teachable. Teaching is otherwise arrogance and mere presumption. Humility is paramount. The teacher must first and foremost be a student. A receptacle. It is only once wisdom, beauty, and grace are received that then and only then does one have something truly worth sharing. It is grace *first*, receiving *first*, that then we can have the courage to give.

Lao Tzu once said: "Other people have what they need; I alone possess nothing. . . . I am like an idiot, my mind is so empty. Other people are bright; I alone am dark. Other people are sharper; I alone am dull. Other people have a purpose; I alone don't know. I drift like a wave on the ocean, I blow as aimless as the wind. I am different from ordinary people. I drink from the Great Mother's breasts."[9]

"I am different," says Lao Tzu. Indeed, he is very different in this "possessing nothing" and being "like an idiot my mind is so empty." Though he is self-avowedly devoid of any particular purpose, his possessing nothing serves a purpose: being empty allows him to receive. He receives the gift of the essential Mother's milk. Lao Tzu says it is possible to receive like this when we practice being empty.

"Look at a window," says Chuang Tzu. "It is nothing but a hole in the wall, but because of it the whole room is full of light. So when the faculties are empty, the heart is full of light. Being full of light it becomes an influence by which others are secretly transformed."[10]

Practice doing nothing, being empty. Do it a few times today. Notice the difference. If you've ever felt empty remember that is only one side to the phenomenon. There is more. Emptiness is a gift.

9. Lao Tzu, *Tao Te Ching*, 20.

10. Merton, *The Way of Chuang Tzu*, 53.

BIBLIOGRAPHY

Auden, W. H. *The Age of Anxiety: A Baroque Eclogue*. Princeton: Princeton University Press, 2011.

———. *The Sea and the Mirror: A Commentary on Shakespeare's* The Tempest. Princeton: Princeton University Press, 2003.

Augustine. *Of True Religion*. Translated by John H. S. Burleigh. Washington, DC: Henry Regnery Company, 1959.

Auten, David Arthur. *Embrace: Strangeness, Mediocrity, and the Living God*. Portland: Inkwater, 2009.

Bonhoeffer, Dietrich. *Letters and Papers from Prison*, edited by Eberhard Bethge. New York: Macmillan and Co., 1972.

———. *Life Together: A Discussion of Christian Fellowship*. New York: Harper & Row, 1954.

Brodsky, Joseph. *On Grief and Reason: Essays*. New York: Farrar, Straus and Giroux, 1995.

Bunge, Gabriel. *Despondency: The Spiritual Teaching of Evagrius of Pontus*. Yonkers: St. Vladimir's Seminary, 2012.

Calvin, John. *Institutes of the Christian Religion: Volume One*. Translated by Ford Lewis Battles. 2 vols. Philadelphia: The Westminster, 1960.

———. *Institutes of the Christian Religion: Volume Two*. Translated by Ford Lewis Battles. 2 vols. Philadelphia: The Westminster, 1960.

Chuang Tzu. *The Book of Chuang Tzu*. Translated by Martin Palmer. New York: Penguin, 1996.

Close, Frank. *Nothing: A Very Short Introduction*. New York: Oxford University Press, 2009.

Cosgrove, Charles H. *The Meanings We Choose: Hermeneutical Ethics, Indeterminacy and the Conflict of Interpretations*. New York: T&T Clark, 2004.

De Mello, Anthony. *Awakening: Conversations with the Masters*. New York: Image, 2003.

Derrida, Jacques. *The Gift of Death*. 2nd ed. Translated by David Wills. Chicago: University of Chicago Press, 2007.

Eck, Diana L. *Encountering God: A Spiritual Journey from Bozeman to Benaras*. New York: Penguin, 1999.

Gautama Buddha. *Dhammapada: The Sayings of the Buddha*. Translated by Thomas Byrom. Boston: Shambhala, 1993.

Gibran, Kahlil. *The Prophet*. New York: Alfred A. Knopf, 2006.

Joseph, George Gheverghese. *The Crest of the Peacock: Non-European Roots of Mathematics*. 3rd ed. Princeton: Princeton University Press, 2010.

Kaplan, Robert. *The Nothing That Is: A Natural History of Zero*. Oxford: Oxford University Press, 2000.

Keating, Thomas. *Invitation to Love: The Way of Christian Contemplation*. London: Bloomsbury, 2012.

Kierkegaard, Soren. *Either/Or: A Fragment of Life*, edited by Victor Eremita. Translated by Alastair Hannay. New York: Penguin, 1992.

Kundtz, David. *Moments In Between: The Art of the Quiet Mind*. York Beach: Conari, 2006.

Laird, Martin. *A Sunlit Absence: Silence, Awareness, and Contemplation*. Oxford: Oxford University Press, 2011.

Lao Tzu. *The Tao Te Ching of Lao Tzu*. Translated by Brian Browne Walker. New York: St. Martin's Griffin, 2012.

———. *Tao Te Ching*. Translated by Stephen Mitchell. New York: HarperCollins, 1999.

Manguel, Alberto. *Curiosity*. New Haven: Yale University Press, 2015.

Meister Eckhart. *Selected Treatises and Sermons*. Translated by J. M. Clark and J. V. Skinner. London: Fount, 1994.

Merton, Thomas. *No Man Is an Island*. New York: Harcourt, 1955.

———. *The Way of Chuang Tzu*. 2nd ed. New York: New Directions, 1965.

Nault, Jean-Charles. *The Noonday Devil: Acedia, the Unnamed Evil of Our Times*. Translated by Michael J. Miller. San Francisco: Ignatius, 2015.

Nicholas of Cusa. "On Learned Ignorance." In *Nicholas of Cusa: Selected Spiritual Writings*, edited by Bernard McGinn et al., 85–206. The Classics of Western Spirituality. Translated by H. Lawrence Bond. Mahwah: Paulist, 2005.

Norris, Kathleen. *Acedia & me: A Marriage, Monks, and A Writer's Life*. New York: Riverhead, 2008.

Nouwen, Henri. *Bread for the Journey: A Daybook of Wisdom and Faith*. New York: HarperCollins, 1997.

———. *The Living Reminder*. New York: HarperCollins, 1977.

O'Donohue, John. *Anam Cara: A Book of Celtic Wisdom*. New York: Harper Perennial, 1998.

———. *Divine Beauty: The Invisible Embrace*. New York: Bantam, 1994.

———. *Eternal Echoes: Celtic Reflections on Our Yearning to Belong*. New York: Harper Perennial, 2000.

———. *Four Elements: Reflections on Nature*. New York: Harmony, 2011.

Pascal, Blaise. *Pensées*. Translated by A.J. Krailsheimer. Baltimore: Penguin, 1966.

Peck, M. Scott. *The Road Less Traveled: A New Psychology of Love, Traditional Values and Spiritual Growth*. New York: Touchstone, 1988.

Proust, Marcel. *In Search of Lost Time, Volume Five*. Translated by C.K. Scott Moncrieff and Terence Kilmartin. New York: Random House, 1993.

Raposa, Michael L. *Boredom and the Religious Imagination*. Charlottesville: University Press of Virginia, 1999.

Rilke, Rainer Maria. *Letters to a Young Poet*. Translated by Joan M. Burnham. Novato: New World Library, 2000.

Rohr, Richard. *Falling Upward: A Spirituality for the Two Halves of Life*. San Francisco: Jossey-Bass, 2011.

Rumi. *1,001 Pearls of Spiritual Wisdom: Words to Enrich, Inspire, and Guide Your Life*, edited by Kim Lim. New York: Skyhorse, 2014.

Sartre, Jean-Paul. *No Exit*. Adapted by Paul Bowles. New York: Samuel French, 1958.

Schaeffer, Francis A. *The Francis A. Schaeffer Trilogy: Three Essential Books in One Volume*. Wheaton: Crossway, 1990.

Strathern, Paul. *Derrida*. London: HarperPress, 2000.

The Matrix. Directed by the Wachowski Siblings. 1999. Burbank, CA: Warner Home Video, 2001. DVD.

Wilson, Eric G. *Against Happiness: In Praise of Melancholy*. New York: Sarah Crichton, 2009.

Wittgenstein, Ludwig. *Tractatus Logico-Philosophicus*. Translated by Frank Ramsey and C. K. Ogden. Ontario: Broadview, 2014.

Zuckerman, Phil. *Living the Secular Life: New Answers to Old Questions*. New York: Penguin, 2015.